Lost 65.5 hours in Olympic National Park:

My story of survival

Brian Gawley

Second Edition
July 2009

Front cover photograph courtesy of Peninsula Daily News photographer Keith Thorpe
and publisher John Brewer.

ISBN: 978-0-578-03292-4

Contents

AUTHOR'S NOTE

It took me a lot longer to get this book into print than I ever imagined. A lot has changed since I finished writing this in February 2007, which was more than 15 months after being hoisted out of Olympic National Park.

First and foremost is I no longer work at the Peninsula Daily News in Port Angeles. I opted for a change of pace and went to work for the rival Sequim Gazette, a weekly newspaper located about 15 miles to the east, in July 2008. I continue to live in Port Angeles though.

Another change is that since leaving the PDN, I've cut back my asthma medications to about one-fourth of what they were during the events described in this book. I'm not entirely sure why.

My good friend Brenda Hanrahan, so instrumental in my search and rescue, has returned to the Peninsula Daily News, having left the Sequim job she held when I went missing. She works for the PDN's weekly publication, Sequim This Week, not in the daily paper's newsroom.

My editor, Dean Rhodes, also instrumental in these events, left the PDN and moved out of the area although we stay in touch by e-mail. Reporters Andy Binion and Raul Vasquez have left as well but Jim Casey remains.

Henry Acevedo, the PDN's longtime chief copy editor, died of a blood disorder in July 2008 shortly after I left the paper.

The Crazy Fish Baja and Beyond, where I became a minor celebrity on the local karaoke circuit, closed after four years. The Lyre's Club has opened in its place, targeted at the same demographic, although a lot of the original clientele has moved on.

Other search and rescues have occurred as well besides the two I mention in here. I was involved in one of them.

I was hiking the Appleton Pass Trail in July 2008 when I encountered a couple planning to hike to the top and back that afternoon/evening. I managed to talk them out of it. "You couldn't possibly have encountered a better person to talk you out of doing this," I told them. I think terms like "rescue" and "helicopter" got their attention.

We began heading back down the trail and found the hiker I had met on the way up. He had fallen and broken his ankle. I gave him one of my two water bottles, then made double-time down the trail as sunset approached. I reached my car in the dark and drove down the trail access road until I could get a signal on one of my two cell phones to call 9-1-1. Then I stayed in touch with the rangers throughout the evening and the next morning.

I decided against including these later events in the book though. This is meant to chronicle the events surrounding my disappearance, the search and rescue effort and my subsequent physical, mental and emotional recovery as I and others viewed them at the time. Going back later brings with it a different perspective. I guess you could say one can't hike the same trail twice.

Dedicated to that unnamed couple at the top of Appleton Pass and my former editor, Dean Rhodes, who first asked "Where's Brian?" and didn't stop until he got an answer.

INTRODUCTION

W hile I was a reporter for the Columbia Basin Herald in Moses Lake from July 1997 to July 2000, I interviewed the owner of a new paintball business. He said he retired from the U.S. Army Rangers following his second parachute malfunction.

I laughed and said incredulously, "Second?" A "parachute malfunction" is a once in a lifetime event -- usually at the end. Or else you survive the first one and give up jumping out of perfectly good airplanes entirely.

I guess I shouldn't be too surprised. I've also twice laughed in the face of death, teased its dog and drank all its beer.

The first time was in 1967 when I was about a year old and became seriously ill with bacterial meningitis. I was given a 50 percent chance of living and a 100 percent chance of ending up as "a vegetable." The illness left me with hydrocephalus ("water on the brain") and several feet of Teflon tubing that snakes from a ventricle in my brain, down my neck and chest to my abdomen. I had several surgeries on that tubing during the late 1960s that I don't remember and none through most of the 1970s. Then I had nine surgeries performed between December 1978 and September 1992, including four between May and September 1992.

The second time was when I spent three unprepared days and nights -- 65.5 hours by my count — in the backcountry of Olympic National Park from Sept. 11-14, 2005. "Unprepared" is a bit of an understatement. I was wearing a long sleeve microfiber windshirt, running shorts and a French Foreign Legion-type hat and a watch. I had no food but I was carrying a water bottle.

Fortunately for me, the efforts of Olympic National Park, U.S. Coast Guard, Clallam County Search and Rescue, Northwest Helicopter Co., West Coast Search Dogs, Olympic Medical Center and a few dozen other people, including Peninsula Daily News staff, ensured it wasn't the last thing I ever did.

When you travel to the Grand Canyon, you see full-page, four-color advertisements warning you, "Over 250 people are rescued from the depths of Grand Canyon each year...Most of them look like him."

The photograph is of a young, healthy male who also looks as though he's done this sort of thing before. Then it continues, "A surprising majority of victims rescued from Grand Canyon are young, healthy males between the ages of 18 and 40 attempting to hike to the river and back in one day."

The advertisement is meant to put the fear of God in tourons (tourist-morons). It did for me. I paid attention when I hiked the Bright Angel and South Kaibab trails there in March 2005. I brought a backpack with plenty of food and water and turned around when my watch told me I should, even if I hadn't reached my goal.

I guess being closer to home, familiarity breeds complacency.

I knew I could hike the 20.4 miles from the Appleton Pass trailhead to the Sol Duc River Trail intersection and back (assuming I didn't lose the trail in the dark). I'd done other 15 and 20 mile hikes in Olympic National Park with nothing more than what I had with me the day I went missing.

But I didn't know if I could survive one night outdoors — let alone three — with what I was wearing, a water bottle (which I lost after two days) and no food.

The two questions I get most often are "Were you scared?" and "Did you think you were going to die?" The short answers are "At the beginning and the end." and "No."

The answer to that second question might be based upon the survival principle that if you don't believe you are going to survive, you won't. Maybe it was just the typical "It will never happen to me" pathos of denial that allows people to drive like idiots and do other dangerous things.

I don't know. Maybe it was both.

When I mentioned this book to a Port Angeles City Councilman, he laughed and said, "An entire book on three days." Um, no. It's an entire book on 65.5 long hours for myself, my family, friends and co-workers and an entire community, followed by a high-profile rescue, an interview with a Seattle television station, one night in the hospital's critical care unit, two more nights in a regular room, then two months of recovery.

Probably the weirdest part of my entire ordeal that began, oddly enough, on Sunday Sept. 11, 2005, occurred on Saturday Sept. 17 after being released from the hospital.

My checker at Safeway that day, Fritz C., was the same one who sold me the Gatorade and four energy bars I took with me when I left Sunday for the Appleton Pass Trail. He remembered serving me the day I disappeared.

He was one of the many, I was surprised at how many, to welcome me back to civilization after my rather highly-publicized search and rescue. I don't remember if he was one of those who also added never to do that again. But there also were a lot of them. I'm inclined to agree with them.

CHAPTER 1

The old saying is that no one expects to get into an emergency, which is exactly why you should plan for one.

I had been doing "psycho hikes" in Olympic National Park for a couple of years or so before ending up on the front page of the Peninsula Daily News and two Seattle television news broadcasts on Sept. 15, 2005.

My newspaper, the Peninsula Daily News, publishes Sunday through Friday. It covers Clallam and Jefferson counties, which are located across Puget Sound from Seattle in the state's far northwest corner. One of the paper's Friday features is a weekly "trip of the week" column. A lot of newspapers have them, especially those in areas with as many great day trips as this one. This provided a good outlet for my marathon training. I ran my first half marathon in November 2001 at Seattle, then ran my first marathon in Mesquite, Nevada in May 2002. (Yes, Nevada in May. It was in the 80s when I finished.) I ran my first Lake Tahoe Marathon in October 2002. It is a high altitude marathon that starts at 6,250 feet, almost 1,000 feet higher than Denver. It's also about 1,000 feet higher than Hurricane Ridge, a high-altitude destination in Olympic National Park popular with both tourists and locals.

I can be seen wearing my bright blue Lake Tahoe Marathon windshirt as I'm being taken off the U.S. Coast Guard helicopter at Olympic Medical Center. I received that windshirt after finishing -- you don't get the shirt until you finish at that race -- the Lake

Tahoe Marathon in 3.:58:36, a little more than 9 minutes a mile for 26.2 miles at more than 6,000 feet above sea level.

The nurse in the recovery tent where I spent 90 minutes afterwards told me it was one of the four hardest marathons in the country, along with Pikes Peak, Crater Lake and Big Sur. (I was told that's the area you always see in the commercials with the car hugging the mountainside next to the ocean.) Finishing it in less than four hours is my greatest athletic achievement to date (unless you count this one).

Since I live about 17 blocks from sea level and do my training runs on a treadmill at the YMCA (five blocks from sea level), I have to go elsewhere for high-altitude training. I lived in Moses Lake for three years mere blocks from the city's seasonal ice skating rink and seasonal aquatics center and never went to either. I was determined not to let that happen here, especially in an area with so many great places to explore and visit.

So I would combine the "trip of the week" with high altitude training runs/hikes in Olympic National Park. It's why I happen to have photographs of my adventure. I'd brought a disposable camera to take photographs for the feature column. I didn't think the film would survive getting repeatedly dunked in Boulder Creek for three days. Water poured out of the camera when the technician opened it up, but the photographs came out.

I would put on my running shoes, shorts, and long-sleeve marathon windshirt. I had a French Foreign Legion-type hat that my sister bought for me to use on my marathons and other races. I'm a redhead whose parents were born in Belfast, Northern Ireland. Suffice it to say, I have absolutely zero natural genetic protection against sunburn. I also found the hat was beneficial not just for spring and summer races to protect me from the sun but also for fall and winter races to protect me from the cold.

That hat was one of the things that saved my life.

Next I'd drive to the trailhead of a long, high-altitude trail in Olympic National Park. Then I'd try getting up and down the long, steep, high-altitude trail as fast as possible, not necessarily running. I found that trying to run I often went too slow on the uphills and too fast on the downhills. I also didn't want to constantly dodge the rocks, tree roots, holes and other trail obstacles. So these trips usually consisted of fast hiking.

Note the absence of such things as a map, compass, poncho or flashlight, let alone the "ten essentials" that park rangers implore hikers to take with them. The list of "10 essentials" developed in the 1930s since has expanded to about 13, depending upon how you group them. They are a map; compass; flashlight with extra batteries; extra food; extra clothing; sunglasses; first-aid kit; pocket knife; matches in a waterproof container; fire starter; water; water purification tablets; and rain gear.

I won't deny those "psycho hikes" might seem like taking a big chance or an unnecessary level of risk. The very term "psycho" itself implies a certain realization that it is, at best, an extreme undertaking. But I also will note that many others do such minimally-prepared training runs on a regular basis. I saw one such individual when I hiked up to the 10,776-foot summit of Mount Rose southwest of Reno, Nevada about four weeks after getting out of the hospital. (He was in great shape but wearing running shorts, that's it. Really.) Drivers also frequently travel long distances or over mountain passes without essential emergency items in the car.

They probably just leave earlier in the day. They probably also let people know where they are going and when they expect to be back. I never gave that much thought, because I never expected a problem and had never had one.

CHAPTER 2

I'm a notoriously late starter on these things. I'm a nightowl, so I usually sleep in past the time one should be starting long hikes in early autumn. But I've always reasoned that it's better to go into these things well rested and prepared rather than sleep-deprived and forgetting something important.

The Saturday night before this particular psycho hike, Sept. 10, 2005, co-worker Paul Gottlieb and I had been over at Dan Erwin's house.

Paul was the one who talked me into taking the Peninsula Daily News reporter job. We also had sung karaoke together at various local hangouts since I arrived in Port Angeles in July 2001.

Dan was my first karaoke deejay in Port Angeles at a tavern called The Wreck, during my two-day "tryout" (a sort of on-the-job interview) for the PDN reporter job in June 2001. The three of us were taking turns on Dan's home karaoke equipment until about midnight. When Dan heard I was missing, he was shocked since I had been over at his house the night before.

The last song I did was "Where Everybody Knows Your Name," the theme song from the television series "Cheers." I was hoping Dan had the full version of the song, it's one of my favorites. It was heard on the air only once, during the series' final episode in May 1993. That's a shame because a couple of the verses are rather amusing:

"All those nights when you've got no lights,
The check is in the mail;
And your little angel
Hung the cat up by its tail;
And your third fiancé didn't show;"
"Roll out of bed, Mr. Coffee's dead;
The morning's looking bright;
And your shrink ran off to Europe,
And didn't even write;
And your husband wants to be a girl;"

Unfortunately, Dan didn't have the full version. So I sang the shortened version, then Paul and I left for the night. Paul departed the next morning for a vacation to New York City. He was from central New Jersey, so he was going back to visit friends.

After co-workers determined I was missing, Paul was on his cellphone from New York City with Olympic National Park Ranger Aaron Titus until almost midnight. He said I mentioned something about going hiking on Sunday at Appleton Pass. When Titus called him back Wednesday to say I'd been located, Paul and his friend Joe were in the lobby of the Empire State Building.

After Paul and I left Dan's house, I stayed up a little later then went to bed. I woke up mid- to late morning on Sunday, which happened to be Sept. 11. Yes, it was Sept. 11, 2005, the fourth anniversary of the terrorist attacks on New York City and Washington, D.C. It was pure coincidence, of course, but I was surprised at the depth of people's reaction when I told them that later. Now that date is memorable, to some people at least, for two reasons.

I had my usual breakfast of two sandwiches with slices of chicken breast, fried egg, cheese and tomato. Then I set my VCR to record the Seattle Seahawks playing against the Jacksonville Jaguars and filled my quart water bottle with Gatorade.

I drove to the Safeway store to buy four energy bars and get my morning coffee, which actually is 16 ounces of coffee with one or two shots of espresso. Yeah, I know caffeine, especially that much caffeine, is a diuretic but I need the boost in the morning and I usually hydrate sufficiently before these endeavors.

Then I drove to the Chevron station by the pawn shop to buy a muffin for energy. It was one of those 650-calorie ones that I wouldn't dare eat unless I was about to do something to burn it off. I ate it while sitting in my car by the gas pumps. This was captured on the station's security cameras, which were reviewed later by Ranger Titus during his investigation.

I drove westbound on U.S. Highway 101 and turned left onto Olympic Hot Springs Road. It was a rather nice day, which you could see in several of the photographs I took during the hike that had too much sunlight in them.

The Appleton Pass trailhead is located a little more than five miles bey1ond the Elwha ranger station, about 15 miles southwest of Port Angeles in Olympic National Park. I stopped at the entrance fee station and showed my annual park pass to the entrance station ranger, Lynn Bawden. He commented that it expired at the end of the month.

Despite being so seemingly under-equipped, there is a rather elaborate ritual I go through prior to these "psycho hikes." I guess that's what Ranger Titus meant when he wrote in his report that I was meticulous and very organized. That sure was a surprise to me.

When I arrived at the trailhead, I took off my jeans, put on my running shorts and put my wallet and 1 car keys underneath the car seat. I had my bright blue Lake Tahoe Marathon windshirt on but also had a shirt to change into when I returned. I took off my Jackie Stewart-style cap and put on my French Foreign-style hat.

Then I changed into the $100 pair of running shoes our newspaper's publisher, John Brewer, had bought for me to run the North Olympic Discovery Marathon from Sequim to Port Angeles in June. It was the first $100 pair of running shoes I'd ever owned. They were very comfortable. I put my other shoes behind the driver's seat.

I stuffed four paper towels and four energy bars in my pockets. Then I took one or two Pepto-Bismol to keep my stomach calm. I take one generic Prilosec in the morning but prior to something this strenuous I always bring a backup.

I took two sprays of Nasacort in each nostril. I had surgery in January 2001 to fix a deviated septum I'd had for about 25 years, possibly since that bee flew up my nose. The results were unbelievable. I no longer have perpetual runny noses combined with congested sinuses that inevitably lead to ear infections. I also no longer need to carry large numbers of paper towels or tissues on me. But I still have to take the Nasacort to keep the polyps from growing back.

Next I took two puffs of my Albuterol inhaler, followed by two puffs of my Flovent inhaler. I had been using Albuterol, off and on, for about two years or so, mostly when I was sick or about to go running or hiking.

I don't know if I have asthma, exercise-induced asthma, bronchitis or something else. My family doctor, Dr. Richard Oakes, thinks I have asthma but the respiratory therapist I went to said I didn't. I hate to think that I'm from my father's side of the family and yet also have a condition that runs rampant through my mother's side of the family.

I've finally reached the point where I don't care about labeling my condition. I just want to control the symptoms. So I use the Albuterol. Dr. Larry Gordon had added the Flovent just a couple of weeks before. It acted more to control symptoms versus the Albuterol, which often was used after the onset of symptoms. Then I put on a nasal strip to stretch my nasal passages.

I stepped out of the car and left the left rear door unlocked. I wasn't taking my keys with me but needed to get back into the car when I returned. Doing long trail runs with no backpack wasn't the only calculated risk I took on these trips. But I never was questioned about that. I suppose if my car had been stolen or broken into I would have been.

I filled my water bottle with the red-colored Gatorade I had bought at the gas station. I left one empty water bottle in the car. I left another half-full to drink when I returned.

Then I put on BodyGlide to prevent chaffing. I double-checked the trail on the Olympic National Park map that tells you not to use it for hiking. I drew a crude depiction of the trail's meander with a couple of landmarks and mileage points on a sheet of paper and put it in my pocket. I tore off some orange trail marking from the roll I had and unwrapped the disposable camera. I stuffed them both in the pockets of my running shorts.

I had my company cellular telephone with me but left it in the car. I doubt it *f*would have worked out in those woods anyway. It also wasn't mine to lose, drop or otherwise damage, and besides I would be OK. I always had been before.

I finally was ready to go at about 2 p.m. This was pushing it but I'd come out all right before.

CHAPTER 3

The Appleton Pass Trail begins at 1,750 feet and climbs to 5,100 feet within its 7.6 miles. Then another 2.6-mile section drops down into the Sol Duc Valley for a total of 10.2 miles, or 20.4 miles roundtrip.

The Boulder Creek Campground and the seven small pools that make up the Olympic Hot Springs are located about 2.4 miles up the trail on the southeast side of the creek.

The "trail" up to this point is an abandoned asphalt road that is easy to navigate in the dark. I had done it before. It certainly is a lot easier than tight switchbacks up a steep hillside through a dense, dark forest.

I reached this point in only 32 minutes, about 10 minutes faster than I had before. This was very encouraging.

Once you pass the Olympic Hot Springs area, you enter the forest in earnest, passing through stands of Douglas fir, cedar, and Pacific silver fir. Somewhere in here I encountered two women who were hiking to the Boulder Creek Campground. I remember telling them I thought that was accessed from a different trailhead but that I wasn't their best source. I hope I didn't get them hopelessly lost.

Continuing westward, the junction with the Boulder Lake Trail is located another half-mile up the trail. A little further up the trail past the junction is a wooden sign telling you it's 4.6 miles to Appleton Pass. I reached this sign at 2:50 p.m., less than 20 minutes from the hot springs. Since about an hour had passed, I began eating the first of my four energy bars.

Next the trail passes by two waterfalls. The Lower Waterfall is located on a short side trail about 10 minutes from the 4.6-mile sign. The Upper Waterfall is located about another 10 minutes up the trail at a foot bridge. Apparently, these waterfalls are rather spectacular and are supposed to be one of the trail's highlights. But I didn't stop to see them, I was headed for the top.

Just beyond the South Fork of Boulder Creek, the trail takes an unexpected turn and begins heading up the mountainside. I spent I don't know how long trying to find the route on the way up. I tied some of my orange trail marking tape around tree branches in at least two places through here. When I found my way past what I thought was the last of those sites on the way down, I thought I was home free.

I returned to the trail in the early summer, about nine months after my rescue, and saw the tape had yellowed but was still tied around those tree branches. It was the dictionary definition of creepy.

The trail becomes steep as it rises up out of the valley, climbing steadily from 2,350 feet to 5,100 feet. It crosses Boulder Creek again on bridges in at least one or two more locations. It was these bridges I would travel up Boulder Creek later trying to find. I found out later these bridges were located on branches off the main creek.

The reason I enjoy these long, high-altitude treks isn't just for the scenery once you reach the high country but also the contrast as you move between the lowland forest and the subalpine areas. I took photographs of not just the subalpine areas but the forest as well, including where the trail emerges from the forest.

Soon the trail crosses a subapline meadow with beautiful wildflowers, then avalanche chutes, and finally switchbacks above treeline. It was on this subalpine meadow on the way up that I saw a herd of Roosevelt elk. I heard them moving before I saw them. My first thought was, "Great, I'm going to be trampled." as I looked for rocks to jump on. My second thought was, "Is something spooking them, such as a cougar?" Fortunately, they moved away uneventfully. I managed to get a photograph or two as they disappeared.

The last half-mile of the trail covers a very steep slope that often remains snow-covered until mid-July but was free and clear in mid-September of this drought-ravaged year. I remember looking up from the bottom of the mountainside and thinking I can't possibly be heading all the way up there. I thought maybe the trail wound around the side of that mountainside and continued towards the backside. Nope. It kept going up and up and up.

Eventually I found myself on the last switchback cresting the hill at Appleton Pass. I bounded up the hillside at about 5:13 p.m. and said, to no one in particular, "Where am I?" I thought I might have gone past Appleton Pass, based upon how long I had been hiking. (I was going more slowly than I expected or realized.)

But this exclamation didn't make the best first impression on the couple camping there. The man scoffed at my plan to do the entire 20.4-mile trail in one day. He also scolded me for not having a map. The woman seemed impressed that I was training for a marathon but puzzled that I didn't have a flashlight or a headlamp.

After leaving the campers I passed the small camping area to the right and then the sign, which I later found to be incorrect, reading "Appleton Pass 6,000 feet." It had taken me 3 hours and 13 minutes to go 7.6 miles, including almost 2 hours and 23 minutes to go the last 4.6 miles. That was a rather slow pace for me, especially given my fast pace earlier, but understandable given the steep trail and backtracking a couple of times.

I had another 2.6-mile section to go to complete the entire 10.2-mile one-way trek. I can't remember if I did the math then. But doing it now, if I had turned around there, I could have easily made it back to the trailhead by sundown at 8:30 p.m. But 5:13 p.m. seemed a little early to be turning around and I wanted to do the entire 20.4-mile roundtrip. Besides I'd done the last part of other trails in the dark.

It was after 5 p.m., so I started on my second energy bar. I still had about a pint or so of my Gatorade left. As I started down the last 2.6 miles of the trail to its intersection with the Sol Duc Valley Trail, I kept telling myself I would turn around if it got too late. I'd done that before when I went did the Heather Park Trail two weeks earlier. That was supposed to be a loop hike along the Switchback Trail and Klahhane Ridge Trail to the Hurricane Ridge Visitor Center. It was about 20 miles total, I'd only gone about eight miles and it was getting late in the afternoon. So I cut it short. But I really wanted to finish this one and besides I was further along this time.

The trail down into the Sol Duc Valley took me 47 minutes to go down and 55 minutes to go back up. That's only 1 hour and 42 minutes, which is rather good. (If all this seems rather exact, that's my point. I may travel unusually light, but I always keep careful track of my progress.)

But at that time of day, at that time of year, it was 1 hour and 42 minutes I couldn't afford. Doing the math again, that's more than half the time it took me to get to Appleton Pass.

I hiked back out of the Sol Duc Valley and reached the top of Appleton Pass at about 6:55 p.m. Apparently those two campers saw me disappear down the trail on the Elwha side, although I didn't realize it at the time. I also didn't realize I had dropped my crude map, which wouldn't have helped in the dark anyway.

I started my third energy bar at 7 p.m. as I was descending from Appleton Pass. I started down the 7.6-mile trail, only 5.2 miles to the asphalt road section, with about 90 minutes to sundown. It had taken me 2 hours and 23 minutes to get here from the asphalt road. I could go faster on the return trip downhill and I also wouldn't be stopping to take photographs. So I was starting to get a little worried, but still figured I'd be OK.

CHAPTER 4

I had successfully completed "psycho hikes" on several Olympic National Park trails, including several high altitude ones similar to this one. Among them were the steep 2.8-mile Griff Ceek Trail, 8.1-mile Wolf Creek Trail, 5.8-mile Hurricane Hill Trail, 9.5-mile Happy Lake Trail and the 6.3-mile Heather Park Trail.

Others were the steep 3.5-mile Pyramid Peak Trail and the 5.1-mile Lake Angeles Trail plus the Deer Park to Obstruction Point (and back, 15 miles total) and Wolf Creek Trail to the top of Hurricane Hill (and back, 20 miles total).

A couple of weeks prior to this hike, I had hiked the Heather Park Trail. That actually began as an ambitious plan to hike the 6.3-mile Heather Park Trail, then another 3.7 miles to the Hurricane Ridge Visitor Center and back down.

I refuse to take my 1991 Chevrolet Cavalier with more than 200,000 miles up the steep, winding 17-mile road to Hurricane Ridge. That car has lasted me for more than eight years since I bought it in April 1998. That's longer than all my previous cars combined. I want it to last another eight years and long, steep drives are not conducive to that. So one of my projects was finding as many alternative routes up to Hurricane Ridge on foot as I could.

Heather Park at the 4.1-mile point on the trail is a modest meadow lacking a sign. So I blew past it to the end of the trail. I was about one-third of the way along the next trail to Hurricane Ridge before I realized it. It was late afternoon and beginning to rain. I was in my usual attire of windshirt, shorts and French Foreign Legion-type hat with a water bottle and some energy bars.

I calculated that I was only about one-third of the way along my planned 20-mile route. I knew I could make it to Hurricane Ridge. But didn't think I could make it there and back, about 20 miles total, in the rain, before sundown. So I cut the trip short and headed back down the trail. I wrote about this trek for my newspaper's Trip of the Week column two weeks before I went missing.

My longest "psycho hike" before the Appleton Pass Trail was the 20-plus-mile loop I completed in July 2005 up the Wolf Creek Trail from the bottom of the Elwha Valley almost to the top of Hurricane Ridge, then back down the valley along the Hurricane Hill Trail.

The idea was to do the hike, then get back to work and write an article for the next day's newspaper. I got a late start and it took a lot longer than I anticipated, especially with having to backtrack to find the trail in a couple of places. I balked at going all the way to the top of Hurricane Ridge due to the time and turned onto the Hurricane Hill Trail, saving a couple of miles. After a little more backtracking, I found where the trail descended from the grassy fields above the trees down into the forest. I still had a lot of daylight remaining since it was July.

The last four miles was along the asphalt road from the Hurricane Hill trailhead back to the Wolf Creek trailhead where my car was parked.

As I passed eight hours and 20 miles, I began setting goals for myself. Hiking to that spot way down the road was too far a goal, so I would aim for that tree or that rock or whatever. Then I shortened that further to that next spot on the pavement. After I'd been doing that for a while, I began counting how many strides it was to that next spot on the pavement. It was two. Two strides. I was aiming two strides ahead. Whatever it takes, I guess.

I finally made it back to my car and arrived back at the newspaper office way past my scheduled arrival time. My editor and a couple of co-workers said they almost had called search and rescue.

But the only real problem occurred in September 2004 during what I refer to as "The Infamous Harvest Moon Hike," my first attempt to do that 20-mile loop through the Elwha Valley.

I hiked the 8.1-mile Wolf Creek Trail up to the Hurricane Ridge picnic area. Then I started up to the top of Hurricane Ridge with the intention of making the loop down the Hurricane Hill Trail, then along the asphalt road back to my car.

It only took me about two hours to ascend the Wolf Creek Trail. Then I started on the relatively short, but steep, trail to the top of Hurricane Ridge. It was getting dark and I wasn't sure where the Hurricane Hill trailhead was. There were signs, of course, but I wasn't about to start trailblazing in the dark. So I turned around and headed back down to the picnic area. (I found out later that I actually did pass the trailhead sign. I thought I might have at the time, but wasn't about to go exploring at that point.)

Then once I reached the Hurricane Ridge picnic area, I couldn't find the not very prominent trailhead off the road for about an hour. I walked back and forth along the paved road past the picnic area trying to locate the trailhead. I had three things working in my favor: relatively warm temperatures, clear skies and a full moon. I also wasn't in the backcountry.

The worst case scenario would have been walking down the road from Hurricane Ridge to Port Angeles (OK, it's 17 miles but downhill), then getting a ride back to my car in the Elwha Valley. But it's not like I could have just gone home. My apartment key was with my car keys back at the Wolf Creek Trail trailhead.

I finally found the trailhead and began my descent about 10 p.m. It had taken about two hours to ascend, so I knew it would take only about 90 minutes to go back down. The sight of the Olympic Mountains bathed in the full moonlight, stretching as far south as the eye could see was incredible. So was briefly running along the grassy hillside under that same soft glow. I was having no problem navigating the trail's subalpine area with the full moon.

As I said, there's something seductive about hiking in the high country. I guess that's why I love Nevada and Arizona. I have to get myself to Colorado.

I worried about what would happen once I descended into the forest though. But the moonlight shone through the trees enough to aid my descent. It actually shone so brightly through a couple of gaps in the trees that my eyes had to readjust after I passed through them. I finally got back to my car at the bottom of the Wolf Creek Trail at about 11:30 p.m. I returned home sometime after midnight. I found out later that bright early autumn full moon was called the harvest moon, hence the trip's moniker.

I thought that was as bad as it gets.

CHAPTER 5

I had left the Appleton Pass trailhead at 2 p.m. and passed the dead bird on the way up at 4:20 p.m. So when I passed the same dead bird on the way down at about 7:35 p.m., I began to get worried. I was descending the trail faster than I had ascended it, but not fast enough.

I normally descended trails in Olympic National Park in about two-thirds of the time it took me to ascend them. So far I was coming down the trail in about 75-80 percent of the time it took me to go up it. I couldn't go much faster because this was the trail's steepest section. I didn't want to trip, slip or otherwise go off the trail. At this pace, I would reach the asphalt road at about 9:30 p.m., an hour after sunset, and the trailhead at about 10 p.m.

I reached the fork in the trail and saw the stick that I had left there on the way up to point me in the right direction. I heaved a sigh of relief and patted myself on the back for the foresight, since I might not have chosen the correct trail fork without that marker. Then I passed the second of my marking tape sites and thought I was homefree. There weren't any more places where the trail was difficult to locate or follow, at least in daylight.

I'd always kind of wondered why I didn't eat that fourth energy bar around 9 p.m. It wouldn't have lasted me for three days, of course. But I would have gone a little longer before getting hungry and it wouldn't have gone to waste. I suspect I was too preoccupied with getting back to the trailhead, then finding my way along the trail, then finding my way back to the trail along the creek. Then after a while, the energy bar became inedible and it became a moot point.

I remember passing by a sign and not being able to read it because of the darkness. I also didn't want to take the time to do so. Besides I knew what it said, or at least thought I knew. I was sure it was the sign telling you it was 4.6 miles up to Appleton Pass. So I thought I was at the 3-mile point of the trail, although I hadn't passed the two waterfalls yet. I had reached Olympic Hot Springs at the end of the asphalt road in about 30 minutes on the way up. I passed that 4.6-mile sign after about 50 minutes. So once I passed what I thought was that sign on the way down, I knew I was only about 20 minutes from that asphalt road that leads down from the hot springs. 20 minutes! But that sign was still another two miles or more away. I crossed the second of those two foot bridges across what I thought was the main stem of Boulder Creek.

Then the trail started its switchbacks up through the dark, dense forest.

CHAPTER 6

Until you get outside the city, way outside the city, off the asphalt and away from the buildings and lights, you don't realize how dark the world becomes, or can become, after the sun goes down.

Especially when you are beneath a canopy of trees.

Although I was rapidly losing my natural light, I was able to find my way along the trail through the subapline areas and even into the lowland forest areas. I crossed what I thought was my final foot bridge and went over a couple of sections of boardwalk across muddy bogs. Then the trail began its switchbacks up the forested hillside.

This is why I originally included the phrase "a cautionary tale" in this book's title. I thought I was about three miles from the trailhead, or about a half-mile from where the trail becomes an easy-to-follow abandoned asphalt road.

If I had made it down to that three-mile mark, I still wonder if I could have made it back to the abandoned asphalt road. That trail winds through the forest and it isn't all that well illuminated even in the daytime.

But I wasn't three miles up the trail. I was closer to between five and six miles up the trail. I went back later and hiked up to the three-mile mark where I thought I'd been that night. Those switchbacks were nowhere to be found. I had been much further up the trail than I thought.

I had hiked in the dark before, even through the forest, such as on the "Infamous Harvest Moon Hike."

This was different.

I don't know if the moon had risen yet by this time. It was scheduled to be full by week's end. But that probably wouldn't have mattered much among all those trees on that steep hillside. I literally could not see my hand in front of my face.

I've had a lot of well-meaning people suggest, with varying degrees of sensitivity, that I should have had a map or compass. (I received three compasses and two maps after I was rescued.) I even had one person propose a GPS unit.

They're missing the point.

None of those things would have done any good in that blackness. Drivers know generally where the road goes, but that does no good when the car's headlights go out. I needed a flashlight or, better yet, daylight. The light on my watch just wasn't doing the job.

I stopped at least twice, maybe three times, then backtracked to the wooden boardwalk so I knew I was still on the trail. I began moving forward slowly. I figured that going slowly was better than becoming lost. It would have been easy if the trail had simply gone up the hillside, but the switchbacks made it difficult to follow.

My heartbeat started to get a little faster now. My resting heart rate is somewhere between 48-64 beats per minute. So if I can feel it beating, it must be beating pretty fast. I took a deep breath, checked my watch and realized it was still relatively early, about 9:15 p.m. or 9:30 p.m. I figured even at one mile an hour I could make it to the asphalt road in about half an hour, assuming I was only a half-mile away.

If I had realized it was possible to wait it out nine hours, I might have stayed there (or in that general area of the trail) until sunrise at about 6:30 a.m. But I didn't think that was an option given my attire and supply of food and Gatorade. Besides I thought I was only about 20 minutes from the last part of the trail.

So I continued forward again.

This is where the total nerve deafness in my right ear began to become a problem. Since it had become too dark to see, I could have relied upon the sound of the creek to keep myself oriented. Normally, when someone yells "Over here!" the sound is louder in one ear than the other. So your brain turns your head until the sound is the same volume in both ears, allowing you to spot the person. It's called localization and most people take it for granted. But I ain't got it. I'm left with this frustrating "surround sound" phenomenon. I can hear sounds just fine, I just can't LOCATE their origin. As I moved through the darkness I couldn't always tell where I was relative to the creek I was hearing. Virtually my only reference point was the boardwalk over the muddy bogs back down the trail. Otherwise, I was in the dark with the sound of the creek coming from what seemed to be all around me.

I turned sideways and began sliding the edge of my foot forward along the trail. I figured that way I could tell when the trail turned for a switchback. Somewhere in here I also enlisted the aid of a walking stick so I could feel my way along the trail. I guess you could call it hiking by Braille. It was a good plan but I started going too fast. I don't why except that it seemed to be working and I wanted to get home as fast as possible. My foot hit what must have been a switchback in the trail and I stumbled down the hillside. The fall itself was not that bad, albeit frustrating. But now I didn't know where the trail was and the brush was too thick to just go straight up the hillside until I hit one of the switchbacks.

I found my way to a boardwalk but I remember thinking that from its length and shape it wasn't the same boardwalk as before. So I couldn't see anything and now I had lost my reference point too.

I knew had recently crossed the second of two bridges. I knew the creek was down the hill. I decided to head down the hill to the creek and follow it back to the bridge when I could get onto the trail.

CHAPTER 7

When you get lost in the wilderness, you're supposed to stay put. Otherwise, you expand the search territory, Chief Ranger Tim Simonds explained to me.

You also put yourself at risk for injury. But I wasn't in the wilderness, I thought. I lost the trail in the dark a mere 20 minutes from where the trail becomes the abandoned asphalt road leading down from the Olympic Hot Springs.

Twenty minutes!

I was sure if I followed the creek, it would lead me to the footbridge I recently had crossed and I would be back on the trail again. I suspect having a plan — however questionable — was what allowed me to keep my head for so long without panicking.

(A therapist I talked to later for post-traumatic stress disorder said the laser focus produced by the survival instinct also can lead to decisions that, in hindsight, don't seem like such a good idea.)

I made my way down to where the forest met the creek. I began easing myself down to the creek area below and either slipped or misjudged the distance in the dark. I hit the ground, bounced and was flung forward towards what was either a log or a rock. It was probably a log. I don't know. I didn't check.

I saw a Discovery Channel program once that said during periods of high stress, your body releases a chemical that actually does make you think time has slowed down.

There must be something to it because time literally did seem to slow down as I careened headfirst towards that log with nothing to break my momentum. My forehead hit, stopping my forward motion. Somewhere in here, one of the stems of my glasses broke as the top of the frames smashed against the log and was pushed back on my head. I was lucky my glasses didn't pith me like a frog in a high school biology class. Then, I'm not sure about the force transfer principles here, my mouth closed — hard. I chipped several teeth and broke a wisdom tooth that later required a crown. I also shifted my lower front teeth somewhat. Fortunately I didn't bite my tongue.

I rolled over onto my back, having lost feeling in both my arms. The remainder of my broken glasses was lying on my chest. My first thought was, "Great, I'm going to die here." My next thought was, "Great, I'm going to lay here paralyzed until I die."

I started repeating out loud, "I can move my legs. I can move my legs." That started to calm me down. I knew I wasn't paralyzed. Then I began flexing my fingers, then my wrists, then my arms. The feeling began to come back to my arms the same way it does after your leg or arm "falls asleep." I rolled over and my now broken glasses fell off my chest to the ground.

My next concern was my head, more specifically my shunt. The Teflon tubing that snakes its way through my brain's ventricles emerges on top of my head before traveling down my neck and chest then disappearing into my abdomen. When I stopped my forward momentum with my forehead, the log didn't directly hit my shunt where it emerges on the right side of my head. (I ended up with a small permanent gash on my forehead one inch from where my shunt emerges.) But the sheer force absorbed by my head, I ended up with a concussion, easily could have dislodged it.

After checking that my shunt wasn't externally damaged, I put my French Foreign Legion hat back on, which helped to absorb the blood from the gashes on my forehead and over my eye. (I had been thinking that at least I wasn't bleeding, which tends to attract predators.)

Then I waited to see if I could feel the eerily familiar sensation of a dull, piercing headache or other symptoms telling me my shunt isn't working properly. Once I realized that was OK, I checked my vision and realized that was OK too. I collected myself, found my walking stick and water bottle and got up to continue my journey to the bridge and the trail. Now that I was out from amongst those trees, I could see fine.

Meanwhile, our chief copy editor, Henry Acevedo, and some other employees back at the newspaper office wondered why I hadn't stopped by for usual Sunday night routine of picking up a paper and delivering a couple of one-liners.

CHAPTER 8

The search and rescue report stated the weather forecast was for mostly cloudy skies with a 10 percent chance of precipitation, a high temperature of 59 degrees at 5,000 feet and mid-30s overnight. The extended outlook was cooler with a chance of precipitation. I was at about 3,250 feet instead of 5,000 feet, but I don't suspect that made much of a difference. Fortunately, there was no wind or rain.

I keep a sweater on my desk at work to deal with a hyperactive air conditioning system that blows cold air all year. I had worn sweaters at my desk throughout the year, including the summer. I began doing all this after enduring repeated lengthy illnesses from October 2004 through May 2005.

So as nighttime dragged on and the temperature began to drop, I knew I must keep moving to stay warm. It was the other reason I kept going besides being what I thought was so close to the asphalt road. I also knew I should try to stay as dry as possible, despite traveling along a creek.

My supply of paper towels was just about used up, so I began to worry about my nose running. But it seemed to be staying relatively dry. This was good because I could keep breathing normally and the snot wouldn't be backing up my Eustachian tube and giving me an ear infection. I also could continue to breathe through my nose. It occurred to me afterwards this probably was an indicator of creeping dehydration. When I was left alone in the hospital emergency room following my rescue, I knew my condition was improving when I had to remove the oxygen tube and blow my nose.

I hadn't started rasping for breath or wheezing as I recently had started doing after long distance runs, which was encouraging.

I also wasn't getting severe stomach pain. I had been on the generic Prilosec for four years to control stress-induced stomach acid that sometimes caused intestinal bleeding. I had had a bloody bowel movement after finishing a 10 kilometer race in Wenatchee in May 2001. I was carefully feeling for similar symptoms, afraid that with this much stress and physical exertion and no food the stomach acid would rip apart my insides.

But despite all that I'm in rather good shape from years of running, although it's been a couple of years since I've finished a marathon in less than four hours. I'd been working out recently by running in the city swimming pool. It simulated resistance training which helped to build at least some upper body strength. It also simulated altitude, which helped to build lung capacity.

I've been a runner long enough to recognize the negative feedback loop produced by dehydration. As you begin to dehydrate, your body sends signals to your brain saying you don't want or need to drink.

I soon decided the risk of giardia or other water-borne diseases in a creek that remote was outweighed by the need to remain hydrated. So I began filling my water bottle out of Boulder Creek. I was determined that when I got out of there (which changed later to when I was rescued), I wasn't going to fit the stereotype of being the lost, dehydrated hiker. It's hard to say how successful I was as I lost my water bottle on the second day.

I had the fourth energy bar in my pocket but resisted eating it. I could feel it molding to the shape of my thigh as my body heat had been making it softer and warmer for the past eight hours. I remembered eating those energy bars that sat on my rental car's passenger seat in the Arizona sun on the way to the Grand Canyon in October 2001. I had enough things to worry about tonight, I didn't need that, too. It was better to go without eating and drink a lot of water than get food poisoning in the middle of nowhere in the dark.

I learned later that eating snow is not necessarily the best thing for survival. Even though it provides much-needed hydration, your body also loses precious body heat melting it. I suspect the same principle applied in my situation with the cold creek water. It wasn't just that though. After a while the cold water was beginning to get, well, boring to drink.

I soon realized my biggest problem at this point wasn't physical as much as mental. The concussion I received when my head struck the log was going to make what was already shaping up to be a long night a lot longer.

I had had a concussion once before, following a relatively minor car wreck earlier that year. I had my lap and shoulder belt on but still was thrown forward and then back in my seat. The aftermath was one of the strangest experiences I've ever had, and that's from someone who has had nine surgeries on the Teflon tubing in his brain. It was as though my brain literally was scrambled. I was in a fog for a day or two afterwards. I can remember driving through Port Angeles along a route I knew pretty well, but not well enough to go on autopilot. I took a wrong turn or two or three. Soon I was driving around an area of the city I'd only written about, the newly developing western neighborhoods. Eventually I found my way again but not before realizing something was wrong. Remembering what I wanted to do next was difficult as was recalling otherwise simple information such as phone numbers and names.

The difference between driving those city streets and hiking that backcountry creek was that I knew where those city streets went. I wasn't entirely sure where this backcountry creek went. I also couldn't afford to be forgetting simple things or what I wanted to do next out here.

The concussion intensified a phenomenon that we've all experienced — the song from hell. It's one that you maybe aren't all that familiar with and often don't even particularly like. But it's stuck in your head and you can't get it out. It keeps repeating over and over and over again. It's usually not the entire song either, just two or three verses.

I had had heard "You May Be Right" by Billy Joel either while I was in the Safeway store or while I was driving to the trailhead. It's never been one of my favorites. I didn't realize it was a Billy Joel song until I looked up the lyrics later. Billy Joel songs are a staple of my karaoke song list but not that one.

> "Friday night I crashed your party
> Saturday I said I'm sorry
> Sunday came and trashed me out again
> I was only having fun
>
> Wasn't hurting anyone..."

> "You may be right
> I may be crazy
> But it just might be a lunatic you're looking for
> Turn out the light
> Don't try to save me
> You may be wrong for all I know
> But you may be right"

It wasn't just that the lyrics were running continuously through my head on what used to be called a loop tape. It was that they had become so prevalent in my head, I began analyzing them.

"This is a really dysfunctional relationship. What is wrong with this woman?"

"She only thinks she wouldn't want him any other way. She needs therapy."

"Why did he drive when she told him not to? He could have been arrested."

"Women always think men are going to change. Why do they keep doing this?"

"Why is the singer encouraging this? This isn't healthy."

I never did reach a satisfactory conclusion to any of these questions. Thankfully, by the time I decided to stop hiking in the dark and settle down for the night, the lyrics had stopped. They didn't start again the next day or the following two nights.

I refer to my ordeal as "when I was in the creek" but I actually spent quite a bit of time the first night hiking through the woods along the shoreline. I intended to just follow the creek until I reached the bridge, but sometimes it was easier, or safer, to travel along next to the water instead of through it. That's how I ended up with myriad scratches, cuts and scrapes on my bare shins. I was distracted from that, though, by the severe blisters on my heels. They hadn't entirely healed from my last hike and now they were getting worse.

I can remember thinking that when I got out of here, I was going to have my walking stick framed. My first editor in Moses Lake said his father had done that with his emergency parachute handle. But I broke at least three before I was rescued. I had one with me when the helicopter arrived but left it behind.

I was determined that when I hiked out that night, I was going to drive to the hospital ER and demand an IV, CT scan and bandages for my legs, forehead and eyebrow. I also kept myself going by repeating that when I got out of there that night, I was going to get a beer, several beers.

I remembered my father talking about plane crash survivors literally dying once they were taken down from the mountainside. That's as far ahead as they were looking, so that's as far as they got.

I remembered reading about a Baatan Death March survivor, Cecil Parrott, who died in April 2004. He talked about lying in terrible living conditions in the POW camps next to fellow prisoners. They would talk all night about how their families had forgotten and no one cared about them anymore. In the morning, these men would be dead.

As I read through the newspaper articles on him, it reinforced what a retired U.S. Marine had told me years earlier when we worked together at Nintendo. He told me about two prisoners of war who would take each other on mental walking tours of various places, to keep their minds fresh and active. He also told me the most important thing for prisoners of war was not surviving the physical torture, but the mental.

I remembered watching a History Channel program where a former World War II POW said some of his fellow prisoners were determined to die as free men. So they died literally as soon as the camps were liberated by Allied soldiers. They were now free men, they had reached their goal.

I knew to set my goal much further down the road than just getting out of the wilderness. I was going to get my life back.

CHAPTER 9

We've all seen the movie scenes of people having mirages in the desert. They stumble desperately towards the oasis, only to find it's not there. Technically, mirages are optical illusions caused by light refraction. The best example is the shimmering highway in the distance on a hot day. What people generally regard as mirages actually are hallucinations.

Whatever.

All I know is I was seeing and hearing people and animals that weren't there, just like that oasis in the desert. It wasn't like seeing shapes in the clouds or a pile of clothes in a dark closet that looks like a monster. That's misinterpreting the shape or nature of existing objects. I was seeing and hearing what appeared to be actual people and animals as I made my way through the woods and along the creek on that Sunday night.

I saw a dog down the creek from me, then another walked up to it and the two of them began wagging their tails. I started yelling to get the attention of the owner. Then I remembered the sign at all the trailheads "No pets, weapons or vehicles." I stopped and hoped I wasn't attracting the attention of a cougar or other predator. (Later I decided they probably were abandoned pets.)

I also saw a boy and his dog on the other side of the creek from me. This dog didn't concern me as much as the other two because it was actually with someone. I waved my walking stick over my head from amongst some trees, which probably would have been impossible to see anyway. I yelled for help and that I was lost and hurt. But I also knew I was headed up the creek to the bridge to get back on the trail. So I didn't stay there long trying to get the boy's attention, which struck me as rather odd even at the time.

Two things the wilderness is full of that I hadn't encountered are wild animals and rain. But then as I was making my way through the woods, I spotted four small furry black creatures. I also thought I saw a large tan-colored animal (the cougar mother?) walking up to them, but I'm sure now that was an hallucination or I wouldn't be here. I stopped and watched them for a while to see what they would do. They just sat there. I changed my intended path and began sliding along a large log to avoid going past them. Then I noticed they had begun following me. They seemed curious as much as anything. It occurred to me later they probably were lonely. I can remember throwing things in an attempt to scare them off. But I couldn't find anything heavy enough or big enough to make any real impression. I couldn't tell if they were following me or practicing their stalking skills. If they were stalking me, they needed a lot of practice. I'd look behind me and, one at a time, these little back furballs would appear behind me. I'm almost sure now they were abandoned domestic kittens, not cougar or bobcat kittens. I wasn't so sure then.

That therapist I talked with later asked me why I thought the kittens were real and the people and dogs weren't. I couldn't answer him at the time. Thinking about it later, I concluded it was because I kept seeing the kittens throughout the night. The two hikers and other assorted people were ones I never saw again. I don't know if that's a sufficient explanation, but that's my story and I'm sticking to it.

I remember seeing what looked like a trail on the other side of the creek. So I went lurching from the gravel bed in the creek over to the opposite shore. I sloshed ashore amid a group of plants that I recognized from my hike up the trail. They had long, thin stems topped with round, flat green leaves. They reminded me of flying saucers. It turned out to be a dead end.

I KNOW I saw two people with knapsacks walking along the trail towards me and saying they were 1.5 miles up the trail. They were quite a bit of the way down the trail from me, but I still could hear them clearly, which also was rather odd.

I did actually find my way to some camping area or something. It was a small clearing with a wooden stake of the kind used to mark camping spots. I should have stayed there for the night. It was actually a pretty good resting place. It sure beat a cold creek.

But I continued down a path that seemed to branch off downhill to somewhere. Maybe I thought it was the path that those two hikers who were 1.5 miles up the trail had taken. I don't remember.

After I fought my way out of that area and back uphill, I went back towards the camping area and couldn't find it.

I kept being seduced by what appeared to be trails. Now I was really beginning to wish I had stayed at that campsite I think I ran across. I wanted to find my way onto a trail, any trail.

As I was making my way through the creek, I concluded that eventually I would have to just walk through the creek instead of trying to rock-hop. This was reinforced after slipping off the rocks a few times and ending up wetter than if I had just walked through the creek.

(Yes, I was only wearing shorts but if I had been wearing pants, they would have gotten wet and stayed wet. Shorts were easier to manage if not really warmer.)

I must have seen a couple dozen people that first night. I don't know if it was being in the dark with no glasses or the concussion or some combination of both. I do know that not a single one of them came to my aid, not even the animals. I also thought I saw the headlights of cars on a road off amongst the trees. This clouded my judgment because something similar had happened to me years ago while hiking back from the hot springs in the dark. I kept moving through the darkness towards what looked like the passing headlights.

The strangest part of the hallucinations, and arguably the most frustrating, had to be the music I kept hearing. I don't know if it was a result of the concussion or some kind of auditory hallucination. Whatever the cause, this music kept leading toward areas where I thought there were campers who could help me. I would go lurching towards one place or another, yelling for help. I don't know why I suddenly decided to trust my ability to locate sound when I know damn well I can't. I can't remember if that occurred to me then.

I kept moving through the dark because I knew I needed to keep my body temperature up in the cold to avoid, I wasn't even considering hypothermia at this point, shivering and just being cold. Eventually though, I realized traveling in the dark was counter-productive. This was driven home to me when I found myself tossing stones at where I wanted to walk to see if there were rocks there or water and if so, how deep. I began realizing that if I couldn't even tell where or into what I was stepping, I probably better stop for the night. So I settled down to wait for daybreak.

I had begun attending yoga classes in early 2005. My repeated illnesses made other forms of exercise difficult or impossible. I also thought the breathing and stretching would help both my running and singing. I went more for the physical benefits than the mental ones. But as I settled down on a gravel bed that first night, I had a nagging knot in the middle of my upper back. So I tried to untie it using some of the relaxation techniques the instructor had shown us. I was only moderately successful.

I kept myself occupied by counting sheep, more or less. I often get to sleep by counting backwards from 5,000. Since the objective this time was to stay awake, I counted up instead of down. I knew from years of running that if I stayed seated all night, my leg muscles would tighten up. Then I would be virtually unable to walk in the morning. So I would sit or squat on a gravel bed in the creek and count off by sets of 100. Sitting was hard on my tailbone and buttocks. Squatting was hard on my leg muscles, especially my quadriceps. I would count fairly slowly and pause periodically, I had a lot of time to kill.

Sometimes I would sing, although I couldn't always remember the lyrics to songs I'd known for years or even decades. Or else I would pause and forget where I was in the song. I would either repeat a verse or two or else start the song over. As I said, I had a lot of time to kill.

I would check my watch after each set of 100 until an hour had passed. Then I would force myself to stand up at the very least, if not take a few steps. The standing and walking could take another 10-15 minutes. I repeated the process, more or less, until daybreak.

Squat. Count. Sing. Count. Stand. Stagger. Fall. Stand up. Stagger. Sit Back Down. Squat. Count. Sing. Count.

I filled my water bottle from small pools adjacent to the gravel bed where I had settled down for the night. Since the water wasn't running, I had to check it in the moonlight for leaves, dirt and other objects.

I also made sure to urinate — I still was doing that — in a different part of the gravel bar from where I was sitting. I was nowhere near civilization but I hadn't abandoned it.

The first night went relatively quickly, probably because it was only one night and it wasn't the full 10 hours of darkness. As I continued my ritual of squatting, counting, singing, counting, standing, walking and squatting again, I began anxiously awaiting the arrival of 5 a.m. and daylight. As teenagers in the early 1980s, my friends and I had been camping numerous times in the Denny Creek area of Snoqualmie National Forest. Dawn always had seemed to break at 5 a.m. and wake us up, ready or not. But that had been in July, it was now mid-September. So 5 a.m. came and went with no daylight in sight. What did come at 5 a.m. though, was "the overnight low." I'd heard the television weatherman use that term for years while growing up. But I never fully appreciated until I lived in apartments where my bedroom was so cold at night, the "overnight low" would literally wake me up.

I swear I could feel 5 a.m. arrive that morning of Sept. 12 even if I didn't already know it by my watch. But the long-awaited milestone came and went with no hint of daybreak. I began my ritual of squatting, counting, singing, counting, standing, walking and squatting again for another hour.

...96...97...98...99...100...

"And the people bowed and prayed
To the neon god they made
And the sign flashed out its warning
In the words that it was forming..."

The brief teeth-chattering episodes were becoming more frequent. When they started I would hold my walking stick level in both hands and begin waving it up and down. I don't why I didn't just wave my arms without the walking stick and save my muscles.

...356...357...358...359...360...

"It's nine o'clock on a Saturday
The regular crowd shuffles in
There's an old man sitting next to me
Making love to his tonic and gin..."

Sometime after 6 a.m. I began seeing the first stirrings of dawn. I knew from watching the sunrise in Hawaii in the summer of 1977, about 3,000 feet lower in elevation, that it would start getting light out long before the actual sunrise became visible. The creeping daylight was encouraging but not enough yet for traveling. Finally about 6:30 a.m. it was fully daylight.

I wish I could describe adequately the optimistic feeling I had when dawn broke on Monday morning. I had survived a night in the wilderness after hitting my head, in running shorts with no food, without getting attacked by wild animals or losing my mind.

The other reason for my optimism was that I concluded I had been going up the wrong branch of the creek. I had passed a sign early on the hike noting the South Fork of Boulder Creek. I concluded I had been going up the creek's North Fork.

I just needed to go back to where the creek had branched off, find the other fork and follow that one. I would be out of here in a few hours and back in the newspaper office that afternoon, after a brief visit to the hospital emergency room.

It's occurred to me as I've been writing this that when daylight broke, I could have simply backtracked to the trail along the path I had taken to get to the creek. Then I could have (more or less) found my way back to the trail and, now in daylight, found my way back down the trail. Maybe.

Back at the Peninsula Daily News office, co-worker Jim Casey questioned my absence as my usual late morning arrival time came and went. But the department head assured him that I had worked the previous Labor Day holiday (I hadn't) and was taking a comp day off.

The three people who would have known that was not the case weren't there. My editor Dean Rhodes didn't work Mondays. Former co-worker and good friend Brenda Hanrahan was gone to another job. Paul was on vacation in New York City.

But soon a lot of people were going to start wondering what had happened to me.

As a local government reporter, I attend a lot of meetings. A lot of meetings. I calculated the average at between three to five a week, every week. The week of Sept. 12-16, 2005 was one of those "perfect storms," to use the cliché.

It included the second Monday of the month, when the port district holds one of its two monthly meetings, at 9:30 a.m. The public utility district also meets every Monday, at 1:30 p.m. I wasn't assigned to cover that Monday's noon luncheon of the Port Angeles Chamber of Commerce.

The week also included the second Tuesday, which is when the city's utility advisory committee has its monthly meeting, at 3 p.m. It was followed by the second Wednesday of the month, which is when the city planning commission holds one of its two monthly meetings, at 6 p.m. Finally, the week also included the third Thursday, which is when the city's parks and recreation advisory commission meets, at 7 p.m.

As Monday morning's port district meeting dragged on, a couple of people questioned my absence. I was regarded as a dedicated reporter and not one who would miss a regular meeting unless it conflicted with another regular meeting.

Then in the afternoon, public utility district commissioner Hugh Haffner also questioned my absence, ("Where's Brian?") although my attendance at those Monday afternoon sessions was more sporadic. He thought I might have gone to a running race that weekend and hadn't returned.

Monday came and went as I continued my trek through Boulder Creek. Some people at the office continued wondering about my absence. But the department head had assured them I was taking a comp day off. So although they were wondering about my absence, they weren't becoming especially alarmed. Yet.

CHAPTER 10

After a day and a half or more of traveling upstream without finding the elusive bridge or trail, I decided to head back downstream. I'd obviously missed the bridge due to traveling too much through the woods and not following the creek closely enough. It also occurred to me that since water flows downhill, I could follow the creek down off the mountainside into the valley. I knew I was in the Elwha Valley and thus the Elwha River drainage. So if I followed the creek long enough, it would lead me to the river, which must have some sign of civilization. I learned later that is exactly the reasoning of 86 percent of all lost hikers. (The creek actually empties into Lake Mills behind the Glines Canyon Dam.)

The new plan worked, at least on paper. When I was spotted at GPS coordinates 47 58 12.6N and 123 42 36.4W, I was about a mile to a mile and a half upstream of the Olympic Hot Springs and only 850 feet off the trail.

But the further I traveled downstream, the deeper and faster the creek became and the steeper and more brush-covered the areas to the sides became. When I was rescued it was out of a steep box canyon with thick stands of tall trees on both sides.

I don't know how much of this was trying to find my way back and how much was the equivalent of exploring the woods behind the backyard. Sometimes I wonder.

By this time, I had abandoned traveling along the shoreline. I thought that being away from the creek had contributed to not finding the bridge. I began traveling literally through the creek, stepping across rocks to the next gravel bar. Fortunately, the area was going through the second-worst drought in 30 years. After a while I realized eventually I would have to step on submerged rocks and otherwise get my feet to make any progress.

I can remember heading further and further downstream on the second day, now wondering if I still was in the park. The terrain had become very rugged with tightly grouped trees that had to be well over 100 feet tall. It turned out I wasn't even close to being outside the park but the area began to look more and more like "wilderness" and less and less like a "park."

The second night (Monday) I realized would be a lot longer because I was settling down a lot earlier. As I sat on the ground, I waved my walking stick back and forth to keep my blood circulating and keep my teeth from chattering.

...134...135...136...

"Hello darkness my old friend
I've come to talk with you again
Because a vision softly creeping
Left its seeds while I was sleeping..."

I probably should have just waved my arms without the stick. Between stopping my forward momentum with my forehead and losing feeling in my arms plus waving my walking stick to stay warm at night, my arms, shoulders, neck and upper back already were sore. Pulling myself up on my walking stick and using my arms while hiking continued to make things worse.

My arms, shoulders, neck and upper back hurt for weeks afterwards. It was Nov. 17, two months after being released from the hospital and several full-body massages later, before all the soreness disappeared. By the second night my leg muscles also were so sore that as I began my 10-hour ritual of counting sheep and keeping my leg muscles stretched, I had to begin pulling myself up with my arms using my walking stick. I would push, pull or drag myself up on my feet, then try to stand without falling over.

Squat. Count. Sing. Count. Stand. Stagger. Fall. Stand up. Stagger. Sit Back Down. Squat. Count. Sing. Count.

This is where all those nights of dirty dancing on Tuesday nights at Crazy Fish became useful. My balance is suspect under the best of conditions. So when I would lift my heels off the floor while dancing, I would periodically lose my balance and go lurching forward until I could put my foot out to stop myself. After doing this for many weeks, I concluded lowering myself back down onto my feet was better than lurching forward. So when faced with a similar situation in the creek, I concluded it would be better to sit back down rather than lurching forward or falling over or down. This prevented more bruising, annoying, potentially dangerous falls.

464...465...466...467...

"Is this the real life?
Is this just fantasy?
Caught in a landslide
No escape from reality..."

...647...648...649...650...

"And now the end is near
And so I face the final -- "
No, bad choice.
"Goodbye Norma Jean
Though I never knew you at all
You had the grace to hold yourself
While those around you crawled..."

By Monday night, although I had been without sleep for more than 36 hours I didn't feel all that tired. I suspect that was the adrenaline. But as I squatted on the gravel bar with my elbows resting on my knees, I periodically would start dozing off. As I began to fall sleep, I would start leaning to one side. This would bring my elbows off my knees and startle me awake again. I didn't mind this too much. Even the tiny amount of sleep felt good. I also knew getting startled awake as I was would prevent me from falling into a potentially dangerous deep sleep. These brief "power naps" helped pass the time too.

Dawn on Tuesday morning was a lot less exhilarating than the day before. It was 10 hours from sundown at 8:30 p.m. to sunrise at 6:30 a.m. It was about another hour before the morning air began warming up, relatively speaking, of course. At about 7:30 a.m., the air temperature and direct sunlight combined to warm me enough to begin my trek again.

As I continued downstream on Tuesday morning, I kept looking towards the shore for a trail. I knew that even if I ended up in the middle of some 20-mile trail leading into the park's interior, I would at least have a chance of meeting other hikers. If I didn't, then at least one direction or the other would lead to a trailhead and civilization. But mostly I think getting back on a trail, any trail, would have given me a much needed sense of hope. I went ashore in a couple of places to follow what looked like trails but those turned out to be dead-ends.

As I was making my way down the creek, I often had to cross back and forth as I followed the gravel bars along the sides of the drought-stricken creek. Sometimes I had to crabwalk across on the rocks. So if I couldn't toss my water bottle to the other side, I would throw it where it would float between a group of rocks. Then I would retrieve it when I reached the other side.

Then on one particularly challenging crossing Tuesday afternoon, I missed the rocks and my precious water bottle began floating downstream. Take that feeling you had as a kid when your ice cream scoop fell off the cone onto the pavement -- and multiply it.

As I watched my water bottle floating downstream I was reminded of the first thing I was told during crisis line training: Don't ever tell someone in crisis that things are bound to get better, they couldn't possibly get any worse. Fortunately my water bottle didn't float continuously downstream and out of my sight. It finally floated behind a group of rocks and sat there bobbing up and down with the current. But it was in an area that was inaccessible without getting my feet really wet.

I had long ago abandoned the idea of keeping my feet out of the water. I would take care to jam them BETWEEN rocks in the stream to avoid slipping. Of course, I had resigned myself to the fact that they would be getting soaked. I counted on the sunlight and my physical activity to keep my feet and my myself dryER and warmER. As I continued hiking, my feet warmed the water and it began to act as insulation, more or less. I can remember one time, I think it might have been Tuesday afternoon, feeling the sun warming my soaked feet.

The curious thing was I ended up drenching my feet but still didn't recover the water bottle. It was stuck behind a group of rocks that were closer to the middle of the creek. It would be easy to say that you've already got your feet drenched, you might as well get the water bottle back. But my feet could only take being submerged in that cold creek for so long. Besides there was no guarantee I could retrieve the water bottle no matter how long I stood in that creek. A little further downstream was an extended stretch of small rocks that created a dry, level walking surface. It lead off towards somewhere that looked as though it might be a way out.

Perhaps the single biggest mistake I made (besides getting into this situation in the first place) was not going back to retrieve that water bottle. I had resolved that when I walked out of there (or was rescued) I was NOT going to fit the stereotype of the lost dehydrated hiker. Whatever else happened, I was going to stay hydrated using my water bottle and the water source I was hiking through.

So I'm not entirely sure why I didn't do EVERYTHING I could to retrieve that water bottle before continuing downstream. It probably was because after hiking through water for two days, I rather enjoyed the respite provided by the extended stretch of small, dry rocks. Since this extended rock bed made for such easier hiking, I figured I could hike down this way for a while and easily return to retrieve my water bottle later. I also knew I was headed downstream towards civilization. So I kept going, leaving the water bottle behind for now.

CHAPTER 11

When Tuesday afternoon began approaching and I STILL hadn't shown up at work, co-workers really began wondering what had happened.

My editor, Dean Rhodes, had Sundays and Mondays off. He arrived at work about 9:30 a.m. on Tuesday, Sept. 13. I had been lost for about 36 hours at that point.

At about 10:45 a.m., Dean looked up and asked inquisitively, "Where's Brian?" Fellow reporters Raul Vasquez and Jim Casey both stopped what they were doing, turned in unison to look at my empty chair, turned back to Dean and said they didn't know. They both said they had been wondering the same thing, especially since I hadn't been at work on Monday either.

"What do you mean he wasn't here Monday? Did he call in sick?"

Monday had been our department head's last day before leaving on a driving vacation to California. He was responsible for supervising the newsroom on Mondays. He had assumed I was taking a comp day off for working the Labor Day holiday. He never called Dean to double-check. No one had called my apartment. Then our department head left later that day or the next morning for his trip to California, assuming everything was fine.

Dean went into our publisher John Brewer's office and asked him if I had called in sick. John said he didn't know. Dean called our department head on his cellphone somewhere in Oregon and asked him if I had called in sick. He said he didn't know but thought I had taken a comp day.

Dean checked the large calendar on the wall over my desk where I noted my numerous meetings as well as other personal appointments. He saw I had two or three meetings that Monday and another for Tuesday. I hadn't marked myself "off" as I usually did if I was going to be gone. Then he checked that morning's paper and saw it had no stories written by me, despite the two or three meetings on my calendar for Monday.

Jim called Port Angeles City Hall and the Clallam County Public Utility District, two places I regularly covered for the newspaper, to ask if I was there or if they had seen me. I heard later that "e-mails were flying around City Hall" regarding my status and whereabouts. A downtown store owner also said the news was spreading quickly by word of mouth through that part of the community. The manager of the 9-1-1 dispatch center, Naomi Riggins, told me months later, "The whole town was worried about you."

Then Jim walked down the street to The Crazy Fish Baja and Beyond to ask the staff there if they had seen me. Crazy Fish, or "The Fish" as it's better known by regulars, is a restaurant and nightclub down the street from the newspaper office. I had been singing karaoke there on Tuesday nights for two years.

I started singing karaoke in October 1999 at Michael's On The Lake in Moses Lake. I didn't realize the lyrics were right in front of you, so I chose a song I knew, The Beatles' "Yesterday." As it was the disc didn't work properly and I ended up singing the first half of the song acappella. After I learned the lyrics were on the screen, I immediately progressed to Queen's "Bohemian Rhapsody," which is as about as difficult a song as you can get.

It was a few months later that the deejay there, Joey, told me I was a good singer. Actually, she told the whole nightclub. After I had finished with Lynyrd Skynyrd's "Freebyrd," she leaned into the microphone and exclaimed, "You can really sing!" I went up to her after the show and asked, "Really?" She said, "Well, yeah, if you'd do more than two songs." (Up to this point I had stuck to "Bohemian Rhapsody" and "Piano Man" by Billy Joel.) So I began expanding my playlist. The rest is history. I became a popular performer. I began getting song requests. Really.

I credit Joey with starting my karaoke "career" that has earned me at least fans if not groupies in three states (Washington plus Nevada and Arizona where I go on vacation.)

After I moved to Port Angeles, I also took three years of voice lessons from Denise McClain. She was the one who taught all the singers who ended up winning contests or performing the national anthem before local events. I credit her with taking my singing "to the next level," as the cliché goes.

Finally, my ability to sing in falsetto allows me to sing Led Zeppelin, which the twentysomething crowd likes, nay, loves. (Although Denise had talked me down out of perpetual falsetto. You can sing up there, she said, just don't live up there.)

All this background had made me more popular on the local karaoke circuit than I had been anywhere before doing anything. I had become a minor celebrity at "The Fish." But everyone knew me by the name I put on my karaoke request slips, "Brian G." I guess you could call it my stage name.

So when Jim asked Katrina, one of the employees, if she had seen "Brian Gawley," Katrina said she didn't know. Then he began describing me and she said, "Oh! Brian G.! No, we haven't seen him."

When I didn't show up for karaoke that Tuesday night as usual, the nightclub staff called the newspaper to ask if I was missing. Apparently, it was a very emotional night at my Tuesday hangout.

Katrina told me later that when they announced I was missing that night, it took the air out of the place. The bartender, Dara, co-owner Cypress and the karaoke deejay Eddie got on the microphone used for the karaoke show. They announced that "Brian G." was missing. They said no one knew where I was and to pray for me.

I talked to a couple of regulars who were there that night. They described the mood as "weird" and "horrible." I was told the crowd conducted "shout outs" to me during the night. I had to "Google" the term but apparently it's a collective show of admiration or respect or concern.

When those leads turned into dead-ends, Jim went to the Port Angeles Police Department and filed a missing person report on me.

Meanwhile, Raul called his wife, Tatiana, to ask if she had seen me or my car around the apartment complex where we both lived. Tatiana knocked on my door and also contacted our landlords Les and Melany West. Melany knocked on my door as well. Raul reported I hadn't been seen around the apartment complex, wasn't answering the door and my car wasn't there.

At this point, Dean concluded, "OK, this is getting weird."

In his 2000 movie, "Castaway," Tom Hanks calculates that he is lost in a search area "twice the size of Texas." I wasn't lost in an area quite that large, but it was arguably more populated than the South Pacific. I could have been in the Seattle area visiting my family. I could have been at any of numerous places on the Olympic Peninsula or in the Puget Sound area at a fun run. I could have been in Eastern Washington. Since I began running in March 1998, I've run races in 27 of the state's 39 counties, some more than others, of course. One co-worker even thought I might have been kidnapped by the enraged boyfriend of one of my many karaoke groupies.

So while I wasn't lost in an area twice the size of Texas, I still was, as someone described it later, "a needle in a needlestack."

Then Dean thought back to a conversation we had had that prior Friday afternoon. Dean was one of those supervisors who would ask you what you were doing that weekend because he actually was interested. He wasn't just making conversation or trying to see if you'd be available to be "on-call."

I told Dean that there was about four weeks left in the hiking season so I probably was going hiking.

Dean called Paul on his cellphone in New York City. Paul told him I had said late Saturday night I was going hiking on the

Appleton Pass Trail but didn't give any more details than that. Still not entirely certain that I was in the park, but with nothing else to go on, Dean called Olympic National Park headquarters at about 1:15 p.m. on Tuesday.

Park staff began questioning him about my appearance, my medical conditions and my vehicle. Dean said he didn't know but he would get back to them. Then someone said our human resources manager, Carol Farquhar, would have all that information in my company personnel file. Dean went into my personnel file and ripped open the sealed envelope containing my emergency contact sheet, which included emergency telephone numbers, physical description, vehicle description, medical conditions and medications. I'd probably filled out one of those on numerous jobs in the past but this was the first time it did anything except sit in a file.

Dean called the national park staff again about 1:20 p.m. and gave them my information. The woman told him she would call ranger stations and have them look out for my car but the park had no reports of overdue hikers.

It was at this point, Dean told me, that everything in the newspaper office "just stopped." Then Dean placed a telephone call that I would not have wanted to hear -- to my father and stepmother in Bellevue. He left an answering machine message asking if I had been visiting there that weekend.

My stepmother Olive said later when she heard the message, she instantly knew something was wrong. Why would the newspaper be calling to ask if I was there visiting?

The investigation continued with John calling former reporter Brenda Hanrahan to see if she knew where I might have gone hiking.

Brenda was from Topeka, Kansas and a 2001 graduate of Washburn University. She also was a big Kansas University Jayhawks basketball fan.

She was in high school when the Oklahoma City Federal Building in neighboring Oklahoma was bombed in April 1995. She was in college when the Columbine High School shootings occurred in neighboring Colorado. Sept. 11 occurred during her first career job. Her friends never did things halfway, she said, such as the one who committed suicide by walking into a lake.

We were the first two, and the only two, full-time reporters on what was supposed to be a four-person staff in the newspaper's Port Angeles office from early July 2001 until early October. We had been on the job for two months when the Sept. 11, 2001 terrorist attacks occurred. That was the longest week of my professional life. I was glad she was there with me.

We worked six days a week until the third reporter was hired in October. I had Saturdays off and she had Sundays off. We would get together on the telephone Saturday evenings and have these long, exasperated talks about our new high-stress jobs for hours like a couple of teenage girls.

We became fast friends.

I survived three unprepared days and nights in the wilderness without serious injury. But when Brenda told me about breaking down every time someone innocently asked her, "Did you hear about the guy in the park?" I wanted to puke.

After she talked to John Brewer, Brenda talked to Laura Rosser, one of the newspaper's special section editors. Brenda and Laura were friends. Laura said I hadn't shown up for work and everyone in the office was debating whether they should call the park.

Brenda's immediate and emphatic response was, "He always does this! Call the park!"

"Maybe he went to Seattle this weekend and just hasn't come back?"

"Call the park!"

"Maybe he went to a race this weekend and just hasn't come back?"

"Call the park!"

Laura told me later that until I was spotted in the creek, she was convinced I had been the victim of someone's boyfriend whose girlfriend had taken interest in my karaoke singing.

Then Raul called Olympic National Park spokeswoman Barb Maynes at home. He said I had not shown up at work and they thought maybe I was in the park. He knew I was not home and my car was not there. He said I told someone late Saturday night about possibly going on a hike in the park. It was unlike me not to show up, Raul said. But it wasn't until Tuesday that they put it together that no one had seen me.

Barb said they take these situations very seriously and to call park headquarters. Raul called and spoke with East District Ranger Dee Renee Ericks.

Raul told Ranger Ericks that I had not left any indication of where I was planning to hike. He knew that I was an avid runner. He also said I was preparing for the Lake Tahoe Marathon in October and liked to run at high altitude.

Raul said I was expected to be at work on Monday. He thought I would plan on a day trip of between 15 and 20 miles, travel light and return to my car. I probably would hike straight up and come back down again, wearing only shorts and a shirt and carrying a water bottle.

Then Andy Binion arrived at the newspaper office. He was our "cops and courts" reporter who would write the news stories of my disappearance and the ensuing search and rescue as well as the beginnings of my obituary. (I heard later that Andy was the happiest person in the newsroom when I was found because then he didn't have to finish it.)

Olympic National Park's dispatch center called Park Ranger Larry Nickey to say there might a missing person in the park. Nickey is the fire and aviation search and rescue coordinator for Olympic National Park. Mine was one of 50 search and rescue missions he ran in the park in 2005.

Nickey said the search and rescue teams and trailhead sentries were pulled in "fairly quickly." Search personnel were beginning to be deployed Tuesday night, with some staying out through the night, he said.

When park rangers began checking trailheads for my car about 3:45 p.m. Tuesday, they didn't have a lot to go on. There had been no reports of overdue hikers. Even the people who reported me missing weren't 100 percent sure I was even in the park. If some were sure, they had at best only a good idea where I might be based upon my conversation with Paul on Saturday night. They needed another challenge.

Park rangers had been given a basic description of my gray, dented, 1991 Chevrolet Cavalier and the current registration information listing the license plates as 846 TOP. But I hadn't put those on the car yet, they were sitting on the front passenger seat. My current license plates read 761 NKE.

Fortunately, an observant park ranger, Kevin McCartney, looked a little more closely. He noticed my "Lake Tahoe Marathon Finisher 26.2 miles" license plate holder. They had been told I was training for a marathon, so he decided to investigate yet further. He looked into the car and saw the gray North Olympic Discovery Marathon jacket on the backseat and then the license plates on the front seat. It was then he realized this was my car. It was the first major break in the search.

Dean told me later that until my car was located at the trailhead, he wasn't entirely sure I was even in the park. He wasn't the only one. Olympic National Park is 933,000 acres. The Seattle area is larger. The Puget Sound area is larger still. This had drastically reduced the search territory.

I didn't know it yet, but help was on the way. It was 5:45 p.m. Tuesday. I had been outside for two days now and faced almost another 24 hours in the elements.

The Wednesday, Sept. 14 edition of the Peninsula Daily News carried the story, "Rangers to search for hiker today: PDN reporter was training for marathon" on page A3. Alongside my company mugshot, it began, "Olympic National Park rangers will begin searching at 7 a.m. today for a hiker missing since Monday."

CHAPTER 12

I was working during Super Bowl XXXVI in January 2002, which featured the heavily favored St. Louis Rams taking on the underdog New England Patriots. Along with just about the rest of the country, I thought the Patriots were going get blown out. I wanted them to win but they were 14-point underdogs. 14 points! I can remember jumping up before the kickoff, throwing open an imaginary barnyard gate and imploring the lambs to flee before the slaughter.

The Patriots won 20-17 on a 48-yard field goal as time expired.

Until I started talking to people for this book, I didn't realize how many people were rooting for me but gave me about as much of a chance as the oddsmakers gave the Patriots. Ranger Titus said he couldn't reveal the contents of the profile interviews he had conducted but that my characterization "pretty well sums it up."

I can't blame them.

One of the newspaper's news assistants, Eva Tallmadge, also was a volunteer on my search and rescue. She said their informational briefing included survival statistics. Eva became wide-eyed as she told me that, based upon the number of days hikers can be lost (three) with what equipment (none), "You beat the odds."

The late William G. Syrotuck was one of the first search and rescue experts to research the behavior of people lost in the wilderness, from children to climbers to hikers and campers. He analyzed a group of 229 search and rescue cases of which 11 percent, or 25 people, had ended in fatalities. Syrotuck concluded that 18 of those who died did so, usually from hypothermia, within the first 48 hours of becoming lost. I was lost for 65.5 hours and outside in the elements for 73 hours.

Jim Casey told me, also wide-eyed, that when he heard what I was wearing, he didn't think I would survive. After I returned to work he even graciously offered, for the bargain price of $50 a day, to refrain from reminding me on a daily basis just how lucky I had been. Brenda said her husband Chris was quiet around her. He didn't think I was going to make it either but couldn't say that to Brenda.

One who did think I would make it was our former outdoors columnist, Darrick Meneken, who was following the saga by Internet and e-mail.

John Brewer said he was told searchers initially were looking on the Sol Duc side of Appleton Pass instead of the Elwha side, which meant they never would have found me.

Andy and Tom Thompson, one of the newspaper's photographers, spent Tuesday driving around the park for the story. Tom took a photo of one of my missing person fliers posted at the Olympic Hot Springs trailhead. Andy said the whole time the two of them kept up conversation about absolutely nothing. They were just talking to keep their minds off the situation. They even started driving to the Sol Duc Hot Springs trailhead on the park's west side instead of the Olympic Hot Springs trailhead on the east side where my car was located.

When Andy went home that Tuesday night, he began writing my front-page obituary because he figured he would be writing it the next day anyway. Writing your own obituary is supposed to be a motivational exercise. You write down all the things you would like to say you accomplished in your life. Then you go out and do them. Most people don't have the privilege, for obvious reasons, of reading their own obituary. It is a privilege, albeit a spooky one. Here's the beginning of mine:

Peninsula Daily News

By Andy Binion

PORT ANGELES - Brian Gawley had a theory.

Depending on the day of the week, the sports season, or whether elections were getting close, Gawley had many theories. But his favorite went like this: There is an asteroid hurling toward earth, a giant one, traveling at mind-boggling speeds, on a b-line for dear Mother Earth. "The government isn't telling us about it, because there's nothing they can do and they don't want to cause a panic," he would say, a wry grin stretched across his face.

Last Monday Brian wasn't at his desk. A dedicated newsman, Gawley, 39, spent his entire life "covering bureaucracies," as he would say, and it was apparent by his steady prose, his knowledge of politics, that his dedication ran deep.

He missed work like the rest of us, for doctor's appointments, to travel across the country to run a marathon. He didn't miss days, though, unless he had a good reason. On Monday, one conscientious person asked "Where's Brian?" But it didn't go further than that.

Andy said later he didn't explicitly say that I was dead because he didn't know that yet nor did he know the exact cause of death.

The killer asteroid theory is my favorite conspiracy theory. It is virtually impossible to disprove and deals not with mere political assassinations but with the survival of life on this planet as we know it.

It's also my way of simultaneously poking fun at conspiracy theorists while reminding myself that we are rather insignificant on a cosmic scale.

I assume, had he continued, Andy also would have mentioned my other hallmark.

After the final out of the World Series every year, I announce the number of days until pitchers and catchers report for spring training prior to the next year's baseball season. (It's approximately Feb. 13.) Then I keep a running countdown. It's usually about 130 days or so. It's my way of declaring "the king is dead, long live the king." Baseball season is over, but next year is right around the corner.

I heard later that co-workers were discussing assembling a search party but the park service was trying to discourage having untrained amateurs involved.

When Dean arrived at work Wednesday morning he thought about me being out there for three nights and thought to himself, "this isn't going to be good."

CHAPTER 13

Once my car was located early Tuesday evening, Olympic National Park rangers began a "hasty search," which is a quick exploration of the trail by six to eight searchers. Paul was upset that a full-scale search didn't begin that night, but park officials made it clear it was late and they weren't going to risk people's lives on my behalf.

Although searchers had found my car, they still had a massive potential search territory. The Appleton Pass Trail I had been on connects to a network that goes to several areas in the park.

Eva, the news assistant, also was a firefighter for the park and participated in my search and rescue. She was quoted in the newspaper as saying if I had taken a wrong turn I could have ended up at the Pacific Ocean.

The ocean was fairly far away but if you look at a map it was a possibility. So "containment personnel" were placed at the Hoh River, Sol Duc River, Barnes Creek trailheads located in the park's western half as well as the Olympic Hot Springs/Appleton Pass and Elwha River trailheads in its eastern half. The containment personnel were to interview anyone coming down the trails.

Ranger Ericks was the incident commander for my search and rescue, which was dubbed OLYM0500000447. Park dispatch called her about 1:35 p.m. Tuesday while she was hiking at Obstruction Point.

Ranger Ericks was notified along with Nickey because the search area was located in her district, which stretches from the park's Elwha area in the northeast to its Staircase area in the southeast. She was told there was an overdue hiker/runner who had not shown up for work on Monday. Park Ranger Kevin McCartney called Ranger Ericks about 3:45 p.m. to say he would be checking trailheads in the Elwha for my car.

Park dispatchers called Ericks about 7:15 p.m. to say that my car had been located at the Appleton Pass trailhead. Chief Ranger Tim Simonds told her to report to the park's emergency operations center to begin planning the next day's search. Ericks met with Simonds, Nickey and Park Ranger Mike Danisiewicz. She worked on my case until 11:45 p.m. Tuesday, then was back on the job at 6:30 a.m. Wednesday.

The park service contacted Grays Harbor Department of Emergency Management Tuesday evening. Their personnel contacted John Watkins of West Coast Search Dogs of Washington. It is a non-profit volunteer search organization founded in April 1985. John had been volunteering on search and rescue missions for almost eight years. His then six-year-old bloodhound Jasmine — she turned seven in November 2005 — had begun training to find lost people at 10 weeks old. They went on 18 searches in 2005, one of their busiest years so far. They already had been on five in early 2006 when I spoke to John. He was told to be at the Appleton Pass Trail trailhead in Olympic National Park between 6 a.m. and 7 a.m. on Wednesday to assist with the search.

Chief Ranger Tim Simonds called Ranger Aaron Titus at home about 7:30 p.m. on Tuesday and told him to come to the Emergency Operations Center. He arrived about 8:20 p.m. and was told to conduct the investigation portion of the search.

Titus had been a park ranger since 1997, the past two at Olympic National Park. Search investigations are his main job. This was the first big search on which he was lead investigator.

Along with being the search investigator, Ranger Titus also is the park's "family liaison." This is the person who deals with the family, including breaking the news when the search doesn't turn out well. Raul had profiled him in this role for a July 29, 2005 feature story. So when Ranger Titus came into the newspaper office Wednesday afternoon to begin looking through my desk, it gave everyone a very uneasy feeling. He said later that maybe he wasn't the best person to be going into the office.

Ranger Titus began a developing a profile of me using a "lost person questionnaire." I had the park service send me a copy. It was eight pages and rather extensive.

The questionnaire asked for the usual information such as name, physical description, clothing, and when and where the person last was seen. But it also asked if the person was familiar with the area, had had any formal outdoor training, medical training or military training.

It included questions about whether the person had any previous outdoor or overnight experience, had ever been lost before, and had ever gone out alone.

One question I found interesting was whether the person was inclined to stay on trails or go cross country.

Then the questionnaire goes into habits and personality. This section gets even more interesting. It asks the usual questions about smoking, alcohol and drug use, hobbies, education and emotional history.

But it also includes questions about whether the person has had past or present legal trouble, shows evidence of leadership, is outgoing or quiet and gregarious or a loner.

Then there's questions about the person's local or fictional hero, whether the person would hitchhike and if so accept rides easily and finally, whether the person would give up, "hole up" or keep going.

During the next three hours, Ranger Titus used this questionnaire to interview several people by telephone, including Paul (twice), my sister Tricia and Brenda. Earlier that evening, Ranger Larry Nickey had called my brother Mike and my editor Dean.

Brenda said that Titus asked her whether I was suicidal. After all, someone who goes bounding up into the high country in running shorts with no backpack surely is suicidal. She assured him that was not the case, this was just typical recreation for me.

She even sent Ranger Titus the following e-mail I had sent to her on Aug. 29 when I did my Heather Park Trail "psycho hike." (I'm more than a little embarrassed about this now.)

"Didja see me on the news? Ya almost did. Got another late start to do Heather Park, Kalhanie Ridge and Hurricane Ridge. It started raining about halfway through, so I turned around about 2:15 into it. (Which was further than I thought, I'm getting faster.) Spent about 40 minutes or so finding my way back to somewhere I recognized. Then it was about 1:45 back down. Fortunately I had my French Foreign Legion hat because I only had my running shorts and marathon shirt. But I did have four energy bars, paper towels and dehydration wasn't a problem because it was so damp. I'm gonna write (part of it) for a trip of the week. Less than six weeks to Tahoe!"

Titus called her back a couple of more times. He had found my plastic shopping bag with various medications in the car and a bees' nest was located along the trail. So he asked whether I was allergic to bee stings as well as about the e-mail. He also called Brenda when I was found.

As Tuesday night approached, I realized I would be going through the entire counting, standing, walking, sitting and counting ritual for a third night. It would be the second full night since I'd started well after sundown on Sunday. It was not necessarily a discouraging feeling. It was more like the frustrated, infuriated, exasperated feeling you get when stuck in one of those automated telephone routing systems from hell. (In his obituary, the inventor of voicemail wanted it made clear that he did not invent those.) Remaining defiant, I kept thinking, "&%$#%@$%$!! not this $#%@$%$ again!!"

Besides, by this point I had become an expert at passing the night in a backcountry creek in Olympic National Park in running shorts.

Squat. Count. Sing. Count. Stand. Stagger. Fall. Stand up. Stagger. Sit Back Down. Squat. Count. Sing. Count.

...345...346...347...348...349...

"Got a call from an old friend
We used to be real close
Said he couldn't go on the American way
Closed the shop, sold the house
Bought a ticket to the West Coast
Now he gives them a standup routine in L.A. ..."

By the third night, not only were the muscles in my legs shot, so were those in my arms and shoulders. So I would pull myself up partway, then turn halfway around so my hands and feet were on the ground. Then I would slowly straighten myself up. If I walked at all by this point, it was baby steps solely for the purpose of keeping the blood circulating in my legs. It was becoming incredibly difficult to just remain standing. I would waver back and forth, using my walking stick to keep myself upright.

My brief naps continued, now more frequently. Fortunately or unfortunately, squatting with my elbows on my knees meant that if I began to sleep too deeply my elbows would slip off my knees and wake me up. I continued to keep the teeth chattering at bay, although it was becoming more difficult. Dawn on Wednesday morning was even less exhilarating than the previous morning. I was relieved I had survived a third night outdoors and it still hadn't rained. But I was becoming mentally exhausted. This was getting old. It also was colder or maybe it was just me that was colder.

I remained determined that I was going to find my way out of here. Once again it was another hour after sunrise before the air was warm enough to continue hiking. I had been outdoors for three nights now. It was time to get the hell out of here and get my life back.

CHAPTER 14

At 7 a.m. Wednesday, the full-scale search began.

It included eight Clallam County Search and Rescue volunteers, seven National Park Service employees deployed as "hasty teams," five "containment teams" to act as trailhead sentries, eight people on the "overhead team" that included a helicopter plus John and Jasmine the bloodhound.

It also tangentially included a psychic, Karen Sandau of Tigard, Ore. She was contacted by her sister, Nancy Woods, who was a former volunteer with the rural fire district that bordered Port Angeles. Nancy swore after a nasty political battle within the district that she would never go on another search and rescue mission again. She went on mine, along with contacting her sister about me. Karen, who had assisted in these situations before, called the park service on Wednesday afternoon to say that I would be found between 2-3 p.m., at the bottom of a cliff with a leg injury. (I don't know what to make of that, but that's what I was told.)

Olympic National Park Rangers Larry Nickey and Mike Danisiewicz conducted the briefing for the search and rescue personnel in park service's Emergency Operations Center before the search began.

One of the Clallam County Search and Rescue volunteers was Ricki McLaughlin. She was a six-year veteran of the county's search and rescue unit and also a special education teacher at Stevens Middle School in Port Angeles. Her classroom was next to that of Patricia Rhodes, my editor's wife. She didn't participate in the search but kept her and Patricia's classes updated on its progress.

Our news assistant Eva stood guard at my gray 1991 Chevrolet Cavalier that remained parked at the Olympic Hot Springs trailhead. She said the searchers received information packets at the briefing that included "very detailed information on you" based upon the profile interviews conducted by Nickey and Titus. (Now I'm left wondering what she knows about me.)

The searchers and sentries were told to ask three questions of people they met: 1) Have you seen this person? 2) Where have you been camping/hiking? 3) Have you seen a solo, male hiker?

Ranger Titus attended the briefing and then accompanied John and Jasmine to the Appleton Pass trailhead where my car was located. He was prepared to break into it, but he didn't have to since I had left the right rear door unlocked with my wallet and keys underneath the seat. Titus took my jeans out of my car and put them in a plastic bag so Jasmine would have a scent to follow.

John said Jasmine is trained to follow only the scent she is given, although she had a problem at the camp area. Jasmine went up the trail to where it branches off to Appleton Pass and Boulder Lake. She started to head up to Boulder Lake before losing the scent. She was returned to the trail junction, picked up the scent again and began tracking me to Appleton Pass. John and Jasmine continued up the trail for six or seven miles before Jasmine began overheating. Dogs' noses can't sniff forever, they have to rest. John reported that Jasmine "was done" at 11:48 a.m. Wednesday. But she was able to establish that I had gone up the Appleton Pass Trail past the fork with the Boulder Creek Trail, John said.

Ranger Titus went through my car looking for clues about my whereabouts or behavior. He saw my Jackie Stewart-type hat, company cellphone, bag of medications and my everyday pair of shoes, size 8 wide with pressure on the outside back. He also saw wrappers from the muffin, antacid tablets, the disposable camera, PowerBars and Band-Aids, along with trail marking tape, nasal strips and empty Gatorade bottles (plus one half-full one awaiting my return).

He said finding my hat, which could have helped witnesses identify me, and my cellphone in the car was "discouraging."

Along with my jeans, Ranger Titus removed my keys and wallet from underneath the seat and the paperwork for my MedicAlert bracelet. Then he left an inventory sheet of what he had taken and a note to call the park if I returned to the car. Then he searched through my wallet and found the charge card slip for the muffin I had bought at the Chevron station. So Ranger Titus went there and reviewed the security camera footage, where he saw me eating the muffin while sitting in my car at the gas pumps. This helped establish a timeline and showed him what I was wearing.

About 1 p.m., Ranger Titus also went to the Peninsula Daily News office to look through my desk. He found maps and photocopies from another hike I had planned but never did. He described the newspaper office's mood as "weird," given his recent profile in the newspaper as the park's bearer of bad news.

Nickey said the weather "wasn't great for flying" and no helicopters were immediately available. The park service had a pilot available for the search but no helicopter. All the park service's helicopters had been out on firefighting duties in Eastern Washington. So the park service got the first one it could, from Northwest Helicopters of Olympia. This particular helicopter was returning from a fire so they swapped out pilots. Park rangers Bruce Klanke and Larry Nickey joined pilot Rob Olmstead in the helicopter at about 1:07 p.m.

At 1:34 p.m., Ranger Barb Kaune's Team 3 radioed that two people at Lunch Lake had identified my photograph as the person they had seen while camping at Appleton Pass on Sunday. These were the two campers I had spoken with that Sunday night. They were the only people I had spoken with on the entire trail except for those two women looking for Boulder Creek Campground. They also would have been the last two people to see me alive. It was now Wednesday and they were still in the park. What are the odds?

They told Ranger Kaune they had talked to me as I ascended the trail around 5 p.m. and then saw me again (although I don't remember seeing them) as I descended back down the Elwha side about 7 p.m. Apparently, I also dropped the makeshift "map" I had shown them which I didn't realize.

This information allowed searchers to focus on a corridor about one mile wide along the five-mile stretch between Appleton Pass and the Olympic Hot Springs.

It had taken 24 hours, a little guesswork, a lot of luck, and a concerted effort by more than 40 people and a bloodhound. But the needle in the needlestack suddenly had become a needle in a haystack. We all know how easy those are to find.

CHAPTER 15

I lived in Eastern Washington twice, three times if you count attending Washington State University in Pullman from August 1984 until December 1987.

Once was for three years and four months from mid-November 1989 until late February 1993 when I was a reporter on the Whitman County Gazette. The other was for four years from July 1997 until July 2001 while working for newspapers in Moses Lake and Grand Coulee.

Eastern Washington is the state's less populated rural half. It presents quite a contrast for college freshmen from the urbanized Puget Sound area who travel over there to attend WSU, myself included.

During those more than seven years (no car in college) I drove all over some pretty remote areas, including dark and snowy mountain passes, without concern. I was worried about crashing, of course, but never about becoming hopelessly stranded.

It wasn't until I had moved to the North Olympic Peninsula that I had a panic attack about being stranded in the middle of nowhere on one of these trips.

I was taking what had become my annual road trip to the Bare Buns Fun Run in Stevens County in late July 2004. It's 394 miles one way — plus a ferry ride, longer without one — from Port Angeles in the state's northwest corner to the Deer Lake area in the state's northeast corner.

I take a loop route that passes through about 11 or 12 counties. After driving through Clallam, Jefferson and Kitsap counties and taking the Edmonds-Kingston ferry across Puget Sound, I drive east along Highway 2 north of Seattle.

The highway passes through a rural area northeast of Seattle before crossing Stevens Pass about 150 miles into the trip. Then it passes through the Bavarian-themed town of Leavenworth and past Wenatchee, which is where I usually make an extended pit stop.

Next is about 60 miles of nothing until the Union 76 station outside Coulee City. I lived in wheat country long enough to know extensive wheatfields aren't nothing -- they are food. But there isn't even that for long stretches through here.

The next 75 miles offers the solace of the small towns of Wilbur, Creston, Davenport and Reardan that break up the mileage even if the towns themselves don't offer much to a weary traveler.

I turn north at Reardan onto State Highway 231, then east again onto State Highway 292 to get to the Deer Lake area. The scenery through here becomes more varied and interesting. But it's still another solitary 50 miles until you reach the Deer Lake area and finally the Kaniksu Family Nudist Ranch where the race is held.

I return by driving south 31 miles on State Highway 231 all the way to Sprague and turning west onto Interstate 90 to Seattle where I catch the ferry back to the Olympic Peninsula.

This time I decided to try saving a little time or distance with a different route. I drove south to Reardan on State Highway 231, then turned west onto Highway 2. I followed that to Davenport, about another 13 miles down the road and turned south onto State Highway 28.

The idea was to follow State Highway 28 west to Ephrata, then take State Highway 283 southwest to Interstate 90. It was different scenery on a route I hadn't taken before and looked a little more direct on the map. It was only 13 miles to the small farming town of Harrington, population 431, then another 24 miles to Odessa. It had more than twice the population, 957 people, and an actual downtown. OK, it was a main street but a business district at least. The town was somewhat familiar to me since I had run a 10k race there in October 1998.

Almost as soon as I turned south onto State Highway 28, I was gripped with this almost overwhelming and inexplicable feeling of terror. I suddenly began thinking — maybe feeling is a better word — that if the car broke down out here, there was nobody around and nobody was going to come around. I was going to die out here — alone and undiscovered.

I don't know why. There was no reason to believe anything would happen to the car. This highway also was not significantly more remote or unpopulated than others I had driven numerous times before, including this trip. I had driven through snowstorms where I probably would have been worse off if anything had happened. None of this seemed to matter.

Maybe it was the solitary house I saw as I turned onto the highway. It was followed not by the familiar wheatfields that would indicate nearby inhabitants, but by long stretches of rugged, deserted countryside.

Whatever the reason, I had this feeling that I was going to get stranded and die out here in the middle of nowhere. So when I completed the 37-mile segment between Reardan and Odessa, I immediately abandoned my plan to continue west along State Highway 28. I stopped in Odessa to collect myself. Then I drove the 19 miles south on State Highway 21 to Interstate 90 and continued my trip westward along a more familiar and well-traveled route.

The afternoon of Wednesday, Sept. 14, 2005 in Boulder Creek was as close as I've come before or since to replicating the sense of terror I felt on that lonely eastern Washington highway.

By early Wednesday afternoon, I had been lost for more than two and a half days. The water bottle I had relied upon not just for hydration but also a food source had been gone for about 24 hours now. So not only did I have to dunk my hands into the cold water for what was a small drink, I also couldn't drink while hiking.

As it got later and later into the afternoon, I began to realize I was lost.

There's a difference between being lost and just not realizing it — thinking the freeway on-ramp is just down this way a little bit — and KNOWING you are lost. The first is just frustrating. The second is demoralizing and, depending upon where you are, terrifying.

We've all heard of the five stages of grief: denial, anger, bargaining, depression and acceptance.

I discovered while researching this book there's five general stages for being lost:

1) You deny that you're disoriented and press on with growing urgency.

2) You admit you're lost, you begin to panic.

3) You calm down and form a strategy.

4) You deteriorate both mentally and physically as your strategy fails to get you out.

5) You become resigned to your plight as you run out of options.

This doesn't say where the kicking yourself stage fits in, but I suspect it's somewhere between forming a strategy and deteriorating mentally and physically.

I don't know if I had reached the fifth stage yet — I wasn't ready to die — but I was rapidly approaching it that Wednesday afternoon. I certainly was well into the fourth stage.

I had been traveling through the creek along a route I judged to be roughly west and east, based upon where the sun was rising and setting. Since that wasn't working, I began to consider going north and south. This would take me up into the forested hillsides. Perhaps I could get to the top of a ridge and see a landmark or even a trail. In retrospect, that was the absolute worst thing to do since there's no way the helicopter could have spotted me amongst all those trees.

It was slow going up those heavily forested hillsides with thick underbrush. I really began to appreciate the people who built some of those early trails. It was in here I began thinking about setting a fire to attract attention to my location. I remembered reading about someone who had done that once. A fire that was started by lightning in the Griff Creek area in 2003 also drew a lot of attention. But then I started thinking that I'd probably end up getting bombed by fire retardant. Three days in a backcountry creek underdressed with no food but I still hadn't lost my sense of humor, or comic tragedy. Besides I had absolutely nothing with which to start a fire in a somewhat damp environment.

I had to clamber over an old tree once or twice to cross a stream or pond. Then I came upon an old rotting tree. I should have realized what that meant before I started across it. I began to feel nagging pains on my shins. They were different from the scratches I'd received thrashing through the bushes, sharper and more constant. Then I realized I was being attacked by brownish wasps or hornets or something. I brushed them off but more were coming. Then I began to feel one fly up my running shorts. I managed to get away from the tree and get them all off me. But not before receiving a very painful sting from the one that flew up my shorts. I still could feel it later that night in my hospital bed.

I abandoned the idea of going up into the hillsides and returned to the creek. I had concluded that following the creek downstream was another dead end. So I began heading back the way I came. I don't what happened but it was as though I had turned onto the Lane when I had meant to turn onto the Street. I was in the neighborhood, so to speak, but not exactly where I wanted to be.

I started making my way back upstream, but I couldn't find the same branch of the creek that I followed downstream. I couldn't seem to find my way back to that extended stretch of small, dry rocks I had encountered on Tuesday afternoon. So I tried going back downstream again. I hit dead-ends in both directions. I remember after hitting both at least twice saying (to no one in particular), "No, that way doesn't work, we've established that."

The shorelines along the creek were becoming too steep to follow. The gravel bars along the shoreline were disappearing. The creek was getting faster and deeper as I moved downstream towards what I was to learn later was Lake Mills.

I've always wondered if things would have turned out differently, either better or worse, if I could have backtracked exactly the way I had come. I suppose at this point that is more than academic. But I thought it strange at the time that I couldn't seem to follow the creek back the way I had come. It was at this point I began to realize I had completely lost my bearings. I already was lost but now I wasn't even sure where I was headed or what I was trying to do.

It was now 2 p.m. and I had wasted almost eight of my 14 hours of daylight without making any measurable progress. I was facing a fourth night in the wilderness with no end in sight. My running shorts were torn and damp. My shoes were soaking wet and hiking through the creek wasn't helping. (The water did provide some relief for my severely blistered heels that still hadn't healed from my last hike.) The water bottle I had relied upon for not just hydration but a food source had been gone for about 24 hours now. I was aching all over and getting increasingly drowsy, either from lack of sleep or hypothermia or both.

But what scared me most of all was I was beginning to lose it mentally. Various disparate images began cascading through my mind, faster and faster. One was Henry e-mailing me the Sept. 8, 2005 story about Steven Lynch, who died from hypothermia while climbing in the Alaska range. Another was that I had nothing left to prove, I was going to cut back from marathons to half-marathons. Of course, there was the obligatory if I get out of this I'm going to start attending church. Another was that I was going to give up hiking. I have a lousy sense of direction and I'm just not cut out for it. I don't really enjoy it, I decided.

Another was the scene from Tom Hanks movie "Cast Away" where his company is glad he's alive and happy to see him back, but his position has been filled. Another was the scene from the 1993 movie "Alive!" where the Uruguayan rugby players stranded in the Andes concluded no one was coming to rescue them and they must hike out on their own. (This, of course, was one of my biggest mistakes.)

I thought about the interview I set up with the Clallam County Housing Authority executive director, which had already been rescheduled once. I thought about the telephone message I had left with the national office of Gottschalks about whether they were closing their Port Angeles store.

I also was trying to remember the CSI episode where the medical examiner talked about "the rule of threes." I couldn't remember it, but I looked it up later: Three minutes without air, three days without water, and three weeks without food.

I began hoping the park ranger who checked my park pass, Lynn Bawden, would wonder why someone who wasn't going camping hadn't driven back out in the evening. (I spoke to him later and he didn't particularly remember me from all the other park visitors he'd greeted that weekend.)

Maybe some observant hikers or campers would notice that my car was still at the trailhead since they had gone up the trail a day or two before and report it when they drove out.

I thought about my co-workers, who obviously would know I was missing. Eventually. But they didn't know WHERE I was missing. That was more than I could say for my family, who had absolutely no idea anything was even wrong.

I thought about the column I wrote for my Moses Lake newspaper shortly after Sonny Bono and Michael Kennedy were killed in skiing accidents that labeled trees as "natural born killers."

In addition to Bono and Kennedy, I noted the numerous anonymous drivers who meet with the same fate courtesy of trees. I also noted that whenever there is an unsolved murder or series of murders, the police always find the body or bodies...in the woods. Hmmm...

I realized this was far scarier than any time I ever was lost in a department store or shopping mall as a kid. It was scarier than getting followed halfway home from the bar by a police car. It was scarier than almost getting hit by a car crossing the street on my bicycle. It was scarier than the Matterhorn ride I was tricked into at the Seattle Center's Fun Forest. It was scarier than the Pirates of the Caribbean ride at Disneyland. It was scarier than the scene in The Wizard of Oz where the Wicked Witch of the West sets Scarecrow's arm on fire after hearing fire was the only thing that could hurt him.

This was worse than losing a job, losing an apartment, having brain surgery or even being chased at night by high schoolers when I was in junior high.

It was shortly after 2 p.m. Wednesday, about 65 hours since I first lost the trail that Sunday night. 65 hours since I knew for sure where I was or what was going to happen next. 65 hours, more actually, since I'd eaten the third of my four energy bars.

I made another attempt to get my bearings. Lacking a compass, I determined the four cardinal directions by orienting myself to where I had seen the sun. I located Klahhane Ridge where I had seen the sun go down, which made that that way west. Then I knew east was behind me, north was to my right and south to my left. Now that I had my directions straight, I could continue.

Then I noticed the clouds that had begun covering the afternoon sky.

CHAPTER 16

It's a funny thing, yelling for help.

I've read that one of the behaviors of lost hikers who reach that final fifth stage is to stop yelling for help, thinking all is lost. It's supposed to be one of those irrational behaviors, along with removing clothing and discarding necessary items.

When you see people in the movies desperately yelling for help, you know it is doing absolutely no good. You wonder why they even bother. Faced with a similar situation yourself, you find that it is instinctive. At the very least, you figure it couldn't hurt.

But it's not that simple.

Constantly yelling for help when there's at least some possibility of being heard is a good idea. Constantly yelling for help when there's absolutely no chance of being heard is unnecessarily discouraging and demoralizing.

When I was seeing dogs and kittens and mirages of hikers and hearing recorded music and thought I was on or near a trail, yelling for help was a good idea. When I had traveled further and further downstream and hadn't seen the dogs, kittens or hikers — real or imagined — for a day and a half now, it was more a sign of desperation than a viable tactic.

Yet, I continued yelling.

By the early afternoon of Wednesday, September 14, 2005, I was standing in Boulder Creek, resigning myself to starting back the way I came, against the current. But it now had been more than

72 hours since I woke up on Sunday morning and about 64 hours since I ate my last energy bar.

I had been tired, physically worn out, for a while now. Now I was beginning to get sleepy. I had been virtually without sleep for three days. I kept stopping to rest and even nap briefly. Along with being unsure of my route, these repeated naps further slowed my progress.

Then I sat on a rock in the creek and began to take yet another hopefully short nap. I remember thinking all this napping was impeding my progress. I learned later sleeping also reduces your core body temperature.

Along with being hungry, thirsty, injured and sleep-deprived, I also was becoming hypothermic, although I didn't realize it at the time. The hypothermia and sleep deprivation probably were beginning to feed off each other.

As I was dozing off, I heard a steady droning. An airplane's droning gets slowly louder as it approaches and then slowly softer as flies away. It's called the Doppler effect.

But this droning was steady. I knew it must be a helicopter, so I labored mightily to pull myself out of my nap. I looked up to see the contracted helicopter from Northwest Helicopter Co.

I stood up and waved my walking stick back and forth with one hand. The two rangers in the helicopter were Bruce Klanke and Larry Nickey, fire and emergency services coordinator and aviation coordinator for the park.

Ranger Bruce Klanke spotted me from the helicopter at about 2:20 p.m. I was told later that Ranger Klanke said he saw a blue tarp. (I was wearing blue shorts and a bright blue Lake Tahoe Marathon windshirt.) Then he said the tarp was waving.

Nickey said it was "almost quite comical" the way Klanke said he had spotted me. "It's a blue tarp. No, it's not. Yeah, it is. Oh wait, it's waving."

Ranger Ericks showed me the digital photos taken from the helicopter and that's about what it looked like. I was told later by Chief Ranger Simonds that they almost didn't see me.

The helicopter hovered for a little bit, then flew off to the north. I thought, "Great, just like in the movies. How demoralizing." Then it circled back and I saw something falling towards me. A bag hit one of the logs lying across the creek just over my head and bounced a few feet away. I pulled myself up and scrambled across the rocks through the creek to it. I opened the bag to find three bagels and a note written on the back of one of the missing person fliers.

The note said if I was Brian to wave my hat. I remember hurriedly, or so I thought, reading the note then briskly waving my hat back and forth. After waiting so long for this helicopter I didn't want it to leave before I could signal, like some sadistic episode of Gilligan's Island. The note also said to stay put, they were sending people and gear to get me. It was signed "Larry." So after signaling to the helicopter I sat back down in the creek to await rescue.

Our news reporter Andy was standing next to our news clerk Eva when the news of my being spotted came over her radio Wednesday afternoon. Barbara Parks, one of our copy editors, said she began crying as she heard the news over the police scanner in the newspaper office. Apparently, my father had a similar reaction upon hearing the news.

I never asked Nickey but I wonder now if the signaling was supposed to serve dual purposes of judging my condition as well as identifying me. Who the hell else would be sitting in a backcountry creek, hundreds of feet from the trail and more than a mile from a campground?

I suspect that might have been the objective because Nickey told me later my reaction time was "horrible." The length of time it took me to react to the bag falling, get over to pick it up, take the note out and read it, then signal to him was indicative to him of hypothermia, Nickey said.

"I didn't think you were being real aggressive in your movements. It took you a while to read the note and react and wave your hat," Nickey said.

I also was standing in a cold creek so that made the hypothermia worse, he said.

I hate to question someone who conducts 50 search and rescue missions a year. But I attributed my slow reaction times to physical exhaustion and being without food or sleep for three days. I also didn't think my response time was that slow, which probably says a lot right there.

Whatever.

Whether the cause was exhaustion or hypothermia, or both, it was obvious I had to be rescued from that creek as soon as possible. I was told later that a debate ensued about how to rescue me, including possibly leaving me out there until rescuers could reach me the next morning. But Nickey told me NO consideration was given to leaving me out there overnight. Sometimes they will drop a sleeping bag or other supplies to stranded hikers who can't be safely rescued until the next day. But that never was considered in my case, Nickey said.

It was a half day hike to reach me and they had only few hours of daylight left. There also was nowhere clear enough or close enough to land the helicopter. The only place the helicopter could have dropped off Nickey would have required about one hour of hard hiking with dead reckoning navigation to reach me.

The park service didn't have a helicopter big enough or properly equipped to hoist me out. It was now about 2:30 p.m., only about six hours of daylight remained. He had to make a decision. Nickey knew the area was within the operating parameters of the U.S. Coast Guard's Dolphin helicopter. (The U.S. Coast Guard is designated as a national search and rescue agency.)

So Nickey requested a Coast Guard helicopter from the base at Ediz Hook in Port Angeles to assist in my rescue. Fortunately, Coast Guard officials had been following the search's progress and offered the use of an HH-65 Dolphin helicopter, one of those big red and white ones.

Since I was on the verge of hypothermia, the impacts of hoisting me into a helicopter were a consideration in how to rescue me. The stress from being hoisted could have forced a lot of blood through my system. This could have caused a dangerous drop in blood pressure that could lead to heart failure.

(And I thought a helicopter hoist was a no-brainer.)

If I couldn't be hoisted out by helicopter, then Nickey would reorganize the hasty teams to meet and take me out on a wheel litter. But that would have taken a lot of time and personnel.

Meanwhile as I sat on a rock somewhere in the Boulder Creek drainage, my sleep-deprived, food-starved brain read, re-read and processed Nickey's note. It slowly dawned on me that there had been a major search and rescue effort on my regard. Knowing help finally was on the way I began to — I don't know if relax is right word — get my hope back. For the first time since dawn broke that Monday morning when I thought I could find my way out, I knew I was going to be OK. But to use both an old cliché and a terrible pun, I wasn't out of the woods yet.

CHAPTER 17

It's fitting that the rescue of a career government reporter had to "go through the proper channels."

The U.S. Coast Guard Group/Air Station Port Angeles is located on the north end of Ediz Hook in Port Angeles Harbor. It is about eight miles from the Olympic National Park headquarters on Park Avenue.

Both Nickey and Ericks spoke with U.S. Coast Guard officials, who wanted to help. The U.S. Coast Guard doesn't like to operate around trees, Ericks said, but does work better at those altitudes. But even though Coast Guard officials had offered to help, park officials couldn't just call the Coast Guard and ask to use one of its helicopters. They had to call the U.S. Air Force Rescue Coordination Center in Langley, Virginia. It is the single agency responsible for coordinating on-land federal search-and-rescue activities in the 48 contiguous United States, Mexico and Canada.

(Nickey told me an informal call was made to let the Coast Guard know the coordination center would be calling.)

Meanwhile I'm sitting on a rock in the creek, eating a bagel and reading and re-reading the missing person flier. It described me as a loner who lived alone and was prone to going off by himself and not telling people his plans. I thought, "Great, now I'm never going to get a date out of this." Three days and nights lost in the wilderness in running shorts with no food, but I had my priorities straight.

I can remember my mind being rather foggy as I read through the flier. I also can remember being amazed, embarrassed actually, at all the effort that had gone into searching for me.

My tax preparer used to work in search and rescue. He told me people who are lost overwhelmingly are embarrassed. He said you have to find people at the point where they are over being embarrassed but before they die. Otherwise, it's not unusual for people to fight with their rescuers.

I was embarrassed, of course. I felt like the person whose car breaks down or gets in a wreck that ties up traffic for miles. Then the person gets home, sees the traffic jam on the television news and slowly begins realizing, "Oh...that was me."

As I was to learn later, that flier wasn't the half of it.

The choice of bagels to give me was an interesting one. I have the same relationship with bagels that President George W. Bush has with pretzels. They have almost choked me on at least one occasion. I thought it would be really tragic if I was to survive all this and then while awaiting rescue choke to death on a bagel meant to help sustain me.

I ate one and then another, which was a little wet in places from the bag being dropped in the creek. Despite being without food for three days, I ate slowly to avoid choking. I didn't get a chance to eat the third bagel before the rescue helicopter arrived. If you look closely at the photograph of me being taken off the helicopter at the hospital, you can see the bag tied around my wrist.

Those bagels were my first solid food since eating my last energy bar on Sunday evening. They also were to be my last solid food until breakfast Thursday morning in the critical care unit at Olympic Medical Center.

I heard the helicopter shortly before 3:30 p.m. I couldn't tell where it was but soon I felt its draft. I'd never realized how strong a helicopter's draft was, especially one that large. It blew my blood-stained hat off my head into the creek, where it remained.

The U.S. Coast Guard's Dolphin HH-65 helicopters have a maximum speed of about 160 knots. This one went about 125-

130 knots on its unscheduled trip north from Tacoma to rescue me. They also are very loud.

The helicopters have a crew of four. This one's crew consisted of Cmdr. Werner Winz, the pilot; Lt. Cmdr. Todd Coggeshall, the co-pilot; Aviation Maintenance Technician II John Neff (Petty Officer 2nd Class); and Aviation Survival Technician III Mikol Sullivan (Petty Officer 3rd Class).

The next summer, the HH-65 helicopters were fitted with newer, more powerful engines and a new control system, giving them a more stable power supply. Then one of them was used to rescue an injured hiker from about 6,300 elevation in Olympic National Park. A Coast Guard public affairs officer was quoted as saying the rescue would have been difficult on that hot July day at 2,000 feet with the old engines.

I was at 3,250 feet on a cool day in September.

Coggeshall told me later the rescue "worked out pretty good."

"We were on a patrol. When we got the call, we were down at Tacoma almost. So by the time we got there, we had burned a lot of fuel. The heavier you are the more demand you put on the engines, so the lighter you are the better."

"We had maybe 280 pounds of fuel at the hospital and about 200 pounds (one-eighth of a tank) when we landed at Ediz Hook. We almost left the rescue swimmer at the hospital to lighten the load for the return flight," he said.

"The trees were, I don't know, 120 feet high. You were down in a gully in a box canyon so it was abruptly rising terrain. We were in a 250-260 foot hover.

"It was unusual for us because it was such a high hoist, 3,200 feet above sea level. We looked at the weight and what kind of engine performance we could expect. We had 245 feet of cable and we ran out of cable," Coggeshall said.

245 feet. That's the height of a 20-storey building. It is also five feet less than the height of the Kingdome, Seattle's multi-purpose sports stadium that was imploded in March 2000. I went

to a lot of sporting events and even one rock concert in that place. I kinda miss it.

Coggeshall operated the hoist from the helicopter's left seat, lowering Mikol down in the creek between the tightly packed stands of trees on either side. When Mikol was still 10 feet off the ground Coggeshall started seeing orange cable, indicating it was about to run out. So he backed up the helicopter and took it down into the box canyon, further amongst the "natural born killers," to get Mikol on the ground.

"The one thing was we were so power limited, if we had lost an engine or had a power failure there was nowhere to go but into the trees," Coggeshall said. That was more or less what Chief Ranger Simonds told me when we spoke after my hospitalization.

I had a firefighter tell me once those dramatic ladder rescues from burning high-rise buildings make for good television but are rare. One reason is that when people take one look down from the ladder, they decide to go down the stairs instead. I realized that just saying, "No, thanks." wasn't an option here.

It also was at this point I realized two things: the full extent of my situation and I wasn't going to convince my editors to keep me out of the newspaper. I didn't know it then, but I had been in the newspaper once already by that point.

When Mikol hit the ground he announced, "Hi, my name's Mike. I'm here to rescue you."

Mikol was 28 years old and had been in the U.S. Coast Guard for four years. He had been a rescue swimmer for more than a year. He also is a certified EMT. This was his first real rescue besides medical evacuations. He was to have his second in August 2006, which also used all 245 feet of cable.

Mikol said later he recognized me from seeing me singing karaoke at Crazy Fish but when he saw me from afar "You looked bad." He didn't think they would be able to hoist me because of a possible neck injury.

Mikol told me later he wished they could take civilians up into the Coast Guard helicopters so I could see what they saw.

Even with the GPS coordinates and knowing I was there, they almost didn't see me, he said.

Mikol also said this was just like an EMT school scenario "but much more intense."

"I think I learned a lot from that. We don't train in a helicopter. It was a learning experience. It was tougher," he said.

Mikol had to conduct a quick medical analysis of me because the helicopter was hovering overhead with him attached and it was low on gas. Since I was moving around as well as moving my head, Mikol decided that a hoist would be OK.

Using a litter or basket would have been the ideal situation but they already were on a mission when they were called so they didn't have one, Mikol said. A basket could have become tangled in the trees anyway, so a "strop augmented pickup" was really the only safe way to go, he said.

He told me to put the harness around my waist. Then he cinched it and asked if it was too tight. I thought, "I'm going to be hoisted several hundred feet through the air. There's no such thing as too tight."

Mikol put me in bear hug, wrapped his legs around mine and signaled to the helicopter. I closed my eyes as I felt us lift off the ground. During the entire journey up to the helicopter, I just kept my eyes closed and silently counted to 10.

"1...2...3...4..."

When I reached 10, we were still in the air, so I began again. I started over again at 1 so the time wouldn't seem so long.

"1...2...3...4..." — then I felt myself, I don't think slip is the right word, but certainly settle a bit into the harness. Now I was really kicking myself for not making that harness "too tight." The hoist was paused to ensure Mikol still had me, then continued.

"...5...6...7..."

I reached 10 for a second time and we were still airborne. So I started over a third time.

"1...2...3...4..." — I felt myself slip or settle again. The hoist was paused again while Mikol ensured again that he had me.

"8...9...10...1...2...3...4...5..." Finally, I felt my feet come to rest on the helicopter landing rung.

This is another situation where words simply fail me. It wasn't just the relief of getting out of the creek but also of getting into the helicopter after being suspended in the air so long.

Mikol lowered me back onto a hypothermia blanket on the helicopter's deck and climbed inside. It was 3:32 p.m. Wednesday, Sept. 14, 2005. I had been outdoors in my running outfit since 2 p.m. Sunday, more than 73 hours.

I was shivering and had goosebumps but was only mildly hypothermic. So Mikol felt comfortable offering me lemon Gatorade for my dehydration. I immediately put my finger in my one good ear. (Did I mention U.S. Coast Guard helicopters are very loud?) Mikol gave me earplugs. Some of the Gatorade went down the wrong way and I began coughing. Mikol offered me antacids or something. I said I was OK. Then I was put onto a backboard and into a neck brace. I've been going to neurologists all my life. I've also researched head and neck injuries for a series of stories I did for my advanced journalism class at WSU. So I understood the need to take the precaution of a neck brace but it also meant I couldn't eat or drink anything more. I was covered with a gray wool blanket and given oxygen. The helicopter's space heater was turned on. It took a mere eight minutes for the helicopter to arrive at Olympic Medical Center in Port Angeles.

For his efforts in my rescue, Mikol received the "Coast Guard Achievement Medal with Operational Distinguishing Device" on April 10, 2006.

A citation accompanied the medal. I asked the Coast Guard public affairs officer to send me a copy.

"Petty Officer Sullivan is cited for superior performance of duty while serving as rescue swimmer aboard HH-65B CGNR 6569 on 14 September 2005. During the early afternoon hours, the Coast Guard received a request for assistance from the National Park Service in Port Angeles, Washington. A lost and possible injured hiker had been located at the end of a box canyon by a Park Service helicopter at approximately 3,200 feet Mean Sea

Level. Due to the rugged terrain and the remote location, neither the Park Service helicopter nor the Park Service ground parties were able to reach the victim. Petty Officer Sullivan quickly readied himself and the helicopter for this unique mission. From an altitude of approximately 260 feet above the victim, he was hoisted to the ground through an extremely small opening in the surrounding trees and dense foliage. Working with utmost efficiency, Petty Officer Sullivan quickly assessed the victim's condition and prepared him for a quick strop recovery. As the flight mechanic hoisted Petty Officer Sullivan and the survivor through the trees, Petty Officer Sullivan worked to shield the survivor from tree limbs and further injury during the long ascent. Once back on board, he continued to monitor the victim's condition en-route to Olympic Medical Center. Thanks to Petty Officer Sullivan's courageous and timely efforts, the victim made a complete recovery. Petty Officer Sullivan's diligence, perseverance, and devotion to duty are most heartily commended and are in keeping with the highest traditions of the United States Coast Guard."

Mikol chased me down later when I was leaving the Castaways nightclub and asked if I remembered him. I'll never forget him. I said that, yes, I remembered him. Then I added a "Thank you." He replied, "Oh, it was my pleasure." Mikol told me later in Crazy Fish that my rescue was the highlight of his career so far. I still meet him periodically at the city swimming pool.

Ranger Ericks gave me a compact disc later with photographs of my rescue taken from the trailing helicopter. I was in a creek that cut a narrow path through very thick stands of trees that had to be at least 120 feet tall. I can remember staring at the photographs later and repeating a breathless "%@%$@.!:"

There's one that shows the helicopter hovering above a narrow opening in a thick forest of towering trees. If you look closely a couple of inches below the helicopter, there's an orange blob that appears suspended in the air. That's Mikol and me. I keep a copy of it on my computer's desktop at work. It's the first thing I see in the morning when I turn it on.

Ranger Titus called Paul back in New York City to inform him of my rescue. Paul and his friend Joe had just come down from the Empire State Building. They were in the lobby. It would have been sometime between 5:30 p.m. and 6 p.m. East Coast time.

I was able to see some of the forest as the helicopter made its way from Boulder Creek back to Port Angeles, about 10 miles as the crow flies. It still was a beautiful area even if it almost killed me.

CHAPTER 18

As I laid there in the helicopter I can remember thinking that, despite my intention that first night to visit the hospital, I was virtually home. I would go to the hospital, "get checked out" as the expression goes, and then go home. Um, no.

As it turned out, I spent three hours in the emergency room, one day in the critical care unit and two days in a regular hospital room, getting released Saturday afternoon. It was Nov. 17, two months after being released from the hospital, before I declared myself free of all the aches and pains and soreness.

The helicopter landed at Olympic Medical Center in Port Angeles at about 3:40 p.m. Wednesday. I didn't know where we had landed. I asked if we were at Ediz Hook, where the U.S. Coast Guard base is located. I was told we were at the hospital.

Keith Thorpe, one of the newspaper's photographers, was there to get a shot of me being taken off the helicopter on a stretcher. So were Dennis Bragg, who ran our local cable television news station, and Darwin Geary, a local stringer for KING-TV out of Seattle.

One of my old newspaper sources from Eastern Washington who saw the news broadcast on cable television asked me later, "Was that you I saw getting taken off the helicopter on a stretcher?"

One of my critical care unit nurses, I was the first patient on her shift, said later that was terrible because there were patient privacy issues. I replied that as a reporter if I hadn't been the one on the stretcher, I would have been right there too.

I was wheeled into the emergency room. Andy and John from the newspaper were waiting to greet me along with Port Angeles Police Chief Tom Riepe and Port Angeles Fire Chief Dan McKeen.

The first thing anyone said to me, I think it was Andy, was the park service wasn't going to charge me for the rescue. That hardly was the first thing on my mind, although it was good to hear. The figure quoted in newspaper stories at the time was $14,600. The final figure was $9,888, not including the time of the numerous volunteers.

McKeen also reminded me that now I couldn't tease him about his becoming lost in the park in August 2003.

I learned later that John and Henry were the source, along with the Olympic National Park news release saying I was not seriously injured, of the myth that I was fine. My co-workers figured I would get out of the hospital on Thursday and then get feted at the local hangout on Friday. Brenda had to explain to them that "not seriously injured" didn't equate to getting back to work on Thursday nor going out on the town Friday night. I was relatively OK given what I'd been through. But the operative word is relatively. I was not fine.

I was started on an IV. I remember the nurse telling me she was putting potassium in my IV, then a tetanus shot. There might have been other things too, I don't remember, it just seemed like a long list. I still was in a neck brace and on oxygen but the backboard had been removed. I remember them asking if they could release my condition. I said yes. I also remember being told they were going to admit me to the hospital.

I gave Ranger Titus permission to give the items he had retrieved from my car, including my car and apartment keys, to Andy. So Andy and Raul were able to drive up to the Appleton Pass trailhead later and retrieve my car.

Andy said the emergency room personnel were "very uncomfortable" with the unprecedented access he and other people had to me. I answered Andy's interview questions as best I could. I also was interviewed by Ranger Titus, who showed me on the map where I had been.

I was in the emergency room briefly before being taken for X-rays and CT scans of my head and neck, then back to the emergency room. Somewhere in here I remember hearing television coverage of the Gulf Coast hurricanes. I remember thinking that at least I still had a home.

Then the emergency room personnel told everyone to leave and pulled a curtain around me.

The wet clothes I was wearing now began to feel cold in contrast to the warm room. It probably was an indication of increasing body temperature. Before it "jumped the shark," I used to watch NBC's hospital drama "ER" regularly. I'd seen them undress emergency room patients numerous times but it's just not the same until you've had it done to you. We've all heard the expression, "Off faster than a prom dress." But that's nothing like what emergency room personnel can do.

My shoes went flying across the room, then what was left of my torn, dirty, soaked blue shorts and underwear. I asked them not to cut my Lake Tahoe Marathon windshirt off me. They were very good about that, although I kept trying to help and they had to keep telling me to just let them do their jobs.

One of the emergency room personnel apologized as she took my temperature with a rectal thermometer. I said after being stung in my shorts, that was nothing. I was covered with a blanket, which was good, because the room was beginning to feel chilly.

I laid in the emergency room for a while with a curtain drawn around me. (That's probably what made me think I was in a room where I would be staying. When they told me I was going to a regular room, I replied that I was already there.)

I was left alone for a while, which struck me as rather odd as this was the "emergency" room. I had fruit juice that I'd been told I needed to drink for rehydration. I had to remove my oxygen tube a couple of times to blow my nose. I thought that was a very good sign that I was rehydrating. I probably dozed off briefly although I was still wired on adrenaline, I don't remember.

When the emergency room personnel returned, electrodes were put on my chest to run an EKG. I heard the woman say my heart rate was spiking up and down too much to get an accurate reading. So that was put off until later. A heart rate monitor was put on my finger.

According to my records, my temperature was 36.3 degrees Centigrade. Normal is 37 degrees. My pulse was in the 90s. It's usually in the 60s. My blood pressure was 138/66, later 126/66, which was rather good considering normal for me is 110/70.

I figured it would be worse. It had been 139/65 when I checked it on the machine in the supermarket pharmacy after a particularly stressful drive to Seattle.

The X-rays of my head and neck revealed the "extensive" sinus surgery I'd had in January 2001 to repair my deviated septum but otherwise were OK. I had had a concussion but my shunt still was intact.

(My neurologist in Seattle, Dr. Steven Klein, was rather upset when he learned of my experience and that he hadn't been notified.)

I had a black eye and gashes on my forehead and over my left eye. I also had cuts and scratches all over my legs, slivers in my hands and severely blistered heels.

Emergency room doctor Tom Tully was quoted in the newspaper as saying that I was lucky. Yeah, I was lucky. Really lucky.

It's not just that I didn't break anything. I also didn't pull, puncture or severely scrape anything. I didn't have any internal injuries. I didn't get poison ivy, although I did have that hornet or wasp sting. I wasn't bleeding except for the numerous scrapes on my shins. The gashes on my forehead and eyebrow had been healing for more than two days now. They hadn't become infected, nor had my shins or heels. I had a black eye but no vision loss or other eye injury.

The doctors' reports said I had no dental injury. I guess they meant I hadn't lost any teeth. I did break a wisdom tooth that required a crown. My four bottom front teeth were chipped and slightly rearranged that also required dental work. One of my two upper front teeth was pushed back slightly.

The reports also repeatedly said I denied having any pain. That was to come later.

I had been OK up to this point, more or less. Then they began piling warm blankets on me. I went into shock and began shaking uncontrollably. I'm sure it looked scarier than it was. I just thought it was frustrating. It was like having full body hiccups. They put more blankets on me but the more they put on me, the more I shook. So they removed one or two. Eventually, I settled down.

"The patient actually is feeling pretty well given the ordeal he has had. His prognosis is good. He certainly may take a few to several days to recuperate from this frightening rather dangerous experience," Dr. Tully wrote in his report.

(My favorite part, though, was "On exam, a cooperative man, talkative, a little hyper almost.")

Then Brenda and Chris arrived about 5 p.m. after getting off work in Sequim. I thought I was doing pretty well at this point, but Brenda told me later "You looked terrible!"

It was a good thing she hadn't seen me when I had arrived 90 minutes earlier.

I suspect the reason for her reaction wasn't just the gashes on my forehead and over my left eye (now bandaged), my black eye, the scratches all over my legs, the blisters on my heels and the slivers in my hands. It probably also was my taut skin and a generally ghost-white complexion and fingernails coupled with severe shaking from shock when they began re-warming me. Maybe it also was the heart monitor, IV bag and oxygen tube attached to me. I also had lost several pounds though virtually none of it was muscle.

Brenda said I was out of it, based upon my responses to the nurses. I didn't seem to know where I was, she said. Brenda and Chris stayed for a little while. We probably talked but I don't remember it.

I finally was moved from the emergency room to the critical care unit at about 6:30 p.m., three hours after I'd arrived. Someone,

I think it was one of the doctors, said to me that I probably wanted to eat a cow. I agreed. But, he said, I was going to be on a liquid diet for now. I asked if the Seattle Mariners baseball game was on television. One of the orderlies said he thought it was over. They had played a 1 p.m. game against the Angels in Anaheim, so it was over. It was the final game of a four-game sweep for the hometown nine.

It was a very comforting feeling to be in that dark and quiet hospital room. I could hear the rain pounding down outside my window. It was a good thing they didn't leave me out there another night.

I was told I needed to rehydrate. So I kept ordering the fruit juice they first had given me in the emergency room. Some time later I had that liquid dinner.

The nurse said I needed my rest so she was blocking calls to my room. I needed people more than sleep, so I told her not to block my calls but she did anyway. Even though I had been virtually without sleep for three days, now I really wasn't that tired. It might have been the adrenaline. It also might have been my elevated blood sugar. Helped by the IV fluids and fruit juice it was 246 milligrams per deciliter when the normal range is 70-110. (My creatine level also was 33 mg/dl when the normal range is 7-20.)

The doctor was concerned about it. I said based upon my marathoning experience that was typical for me after prolonged physical activity and it would return to normal later. It did.

Despite not having my glasses I started watching television. It was Wednesday, there were Law and Order episodes, then the news (including my rescue), then the Tonight Show.

I watched M*A*S*H reruns until 2:30 a.m. Thursday before deciding I should get some sleep. There were more episodes to follow and I still wasn't really dozing off. But it had been 87 hours since I woke up on that Sunday morning, Sept. 11 to begin my hike up to Appleton Pass. So for the first time since Saturday night after leaving Dan Erwin's house, I slept.

CHAPTER 19

I awoke about 9:30 a.m. Thursday to a nurse bringing me breakfast. It was huge — scrambled eggs, sausage, toast, yogurt and oatmeal. Then a nurse took me to the shower room.

The first person to come see me after I returned to my room was Zeller Westabrook, one of the newspaper's news clerks. She brought a small basket of food along with a copy of that morning's Peninsula Daily News.

It included the front page story, "Lost hiker plucked from canyon." It was complete with a full-color photograph of me being taken off the U.S. Coast Guard helicopter, a map showing where I was found and a mugshot.

Zeller also took a picture of me in my hospital bed with bandages on my eyebrow and forehead and a towel on my chest. Then she had Laura Rosser put a digital message on it: "He's alive. He's safe. He's lucky to be alive. We're gonna kill him." My family bought a frame for it. I put it on the mantle I use to display my race awards.

I was told later that despite the concern felt by co-workers during my disappearance (or perhaps because of it), the mood quickly shifted once I was rescued. It became what might be described as one of righteous disgust that I had put them (and myself) through all that. A good translation might be, "Oh, that dumbshit!" Despite the obvious stress in Brenda's voice, I was reassured by her later repeated assertions that I wasn't stupid and that I knew what to do.

John Brewer also stopped by and offered to have the photos developed from the disposable camera I still had in my soaked running shorts. Water poured out of the camera when the technician opened it, but the photographs turned out. Brenda told me later John had taken the ordeal rather hard since he had lost his longtime wife Ann to cancer in March.

I received several telephone calls. One was from KIRO-TV 7 in Seattle. One of their reporters, Chris Legeros, said he wanted to interview me because this story had a happy ending. It was about 11 a.m. and he said they would be there about 1:30 p.m.

My father called and said he and my stepmother Olive and sister Patricia were heading over to see me. Apparently they hadn't left for Port Angeles after my rescue because they didn't know if I would be taken to Harborview Medical Center in Seattle.

I also received a call from Mary Powell. We were reporters together on the Columbia Basin Herald in Moses Lake. Now she was editor of the Sequim Gazette, a weekly newspaper that was a competitor of ours in the neighboring city to the east.

I remember I trying to call Mary as well as Crazy Fish that Thursday morning and forgetting to dial 9 first, so the calls wouldn't go through.

As I sat there in my hospital bed, waiting for the television news crew and my family to arrive, I began reading the newspaper account of my rescue. I stared at the full-color, front-page photograph showing me being taken off the helicopter on a stretcher. I also looked at the map graphic of the area where I had been found.

Then the strangest thing happened. I couldn't wait to try some of the other trails I saw on the map — safely, in daylight, of course. As I said, if you don't understand the allure of the high country, get someone to take you there.

A short time later, the television news crew showed up to interview me. It included Dennis Bragg, the owner/operator of our local cable television news station, his daughter Annie, and Chris Legeros from KIRO-TV.

I'd been interviewed for a newspaper article once but never for television. But I just had a conversation with Legeros and forgot about the television camera. Then I did the same with Dennis. They both were veterans that knew how to get interview subjects to relax and talk with them, not just to them. I think it also helped that I had known Dennis for a few years.

Maybe that wasn't such a good idea though. I ended up telling them about looking at the map graphic and being eager to do future hikes. I don't think I could have sent a bigger collective gasp through the community if I'd announced I was a cross-dressing neo-Nazi.

I received a scolding e-mail from Brenda saying, "Already thinking of future trips, aye? You will bring more gear next time and tell people of your plans, right? Scroll down to the third photo for your answer." She had attached the Web site article from Dennis Bragg's Peninsula News Network that included my hospital room interview.

The third photograph was of me being taken off the helicopter on a stretcher on a backboard wearing a neck brace, skinny and pale as a ghost.

After the interview, Legeros asked me if this experience had given me a different perspective for future stories. I said not really, which hasn't turned out to be true. Now I jump on all the lost hiker or camper stories. It's not just because I know who to talk to and what questions to ask. I also feel this strong connection to my story's subjects and my experience also helps to get loved ones talking.

But I did tell Legeros about the emergency room nurse saying it was terrible to have those television cameramen and newspaper photographers there as I was being taken off the helicopter. There's patient privacy issues, she said. I just told her that if I hadn't been the one on the stretcher, I would have done the same thing.

Legeros told me about getting some background shots for a story about a rockslide that had closed Interstate 90 east of Seattle. Shortly after he and the cameraman left, a huge boulder landed where they had been standing. We swapped a couple of more stories before he left.

Then Dan Gamash showed up. We had lived next door to each other in Bellevue and had been best friends from the time we could walk until seventh grade when I moved a couple of miles away. He went to a private school up the street that was kindergarten through eighth grade. I went to the public school at the end of our dead-end residential street that was kindergarten through sixth grade. That was interesting because when we talked about about our day at school, it was news to each of us instead of just retelling shared events. When I moved across town, I continued going to the same junior high school. So I often would camp out at his house (he often was at sports practice after school) until my ride came in the evening. By eighth grade, I began hanging out with another friend from school and Dan got more involved in sports. I introduced the two of them that summer after eighth grade but that's another book entirely.

It was really weird that I ended up in Port Angeles and Dan ended up in Sequim, only 20 miles away. When he got to the hospital he told me about a hike he just had taken up Mount Muller in Olympic National Forest. Then he suggested we hike the Mink Lake Trail in Olympic National Park, which we did a few weeks later. It was miserable.

Next, Dr. Oakes showed up, which I found surprising although I guess I shouldn't have. I just didn't expect to see the doctor from my clinic in the hospital. He told me about two near-fatal hiking experiences he had had in Olympic National Park.

I was to hear several similar "war stories" later. My favorite was when the Port Angeles Economic Development Director Tim Smith and Port Angeles Human Resources Director Bob Coons were camping at Boulder Lake, close to where I had been, in August 2003. They were sitting around the campfire when two deer went tearing through the campsite, right between them. They looked at each other and started to say that they must be getting chased by a cougar — just as said cougar went tearing through the campsite right between them.

My father, stepmother and sister arrived in the late afternoon or early evening on Thursday. One of the more uncomfortable parts of the visit was when my father and sister left the room. My stepmother just sat in silence, staring out the window until they returned. I suspect she still was upset, although I never asked.

Apparently my then-78-year-old father made quite an impression when he burst upon the newspaper office. Henry thought he was in his 50s, not 70s. Laura said, "He's soooo cute!" and raved about his Belfast accent. (Everyone does that, although I've never noticed having grown up with it.) My father had had quadruple bypass surgery just a year before. He complained in the ensuing year that he had felt better and could do more than before he had the surgery. We all kept telling him that it was major surgery and to give his recovery about a year. Well, he must have been fully recovered one year later because he survived the stress of my disappearance and rescue without literally having heart failure. My father ended up making a $100 donation to a community fundraiser we had in the office.

During my family's visit with me, my father was his usual restless self, off exploring the hospital. So he missed both doctor visits. It was very interesting listening to my sister the veterinarian discussing my test results with the doctor without having to translate the terminology into plain English. They had brought my backup pair of glasses from my apartment so I finally could see again. They visited again on Friday after I had been moved out of the critical care unit before returning to the Seattle area. My sister bought Dean a gift certificate to one of the nicer restaurants in town for his assistance in my search and diligence in keeping my family updated on its progress.

CHAPTER 20

I was going to be OK, but I still had a long way to go.

After I was taken to a regular hospital room from the critical care unit, I had my first opportunity to get out of bed. I still had to use the urinal so the nurses could track my fluid output but now I had a bathroom to visit. Fortunately, I hadn't needed anything but a urinal up to that point. All my hospitalizations and, although I've had a catheter, I've never needed a bedpan. The nurses wanted me to call one of them before getting out of bed to use the bathroom but I didn't. I had a little difficulty standing and walking at first but no more than after many marathons. My leg muscles healed fairly quickly because of all my running.

I wish I could say the same for the rest of me.

My father fell down a short flight (three or four) of stairs onto a concrete driveway when he was in his late 70s. He told me that when you hurt all over, you don't have enough pain pathways to your brain to feel everything at once. So when one area heals, you begin feeling pain in another area that hadn't hurt before. I don't know if that's a correct medical explanation, but that's what happened to me.

The nurse had told me earlier that the doctor had authorized pain medication. I had refused, in part because living with hydrocephalus gives one a high pain threshold and in part because I didn't feel it was necessary at that time. By my second night in the hospital, my other aches and pains had subsided. Now I began feeling all the knots in my neck, back, shoulders and arms that I hadn't really noticed before. When the nurse would ask if I needed anything, I kept wanting to say a shoulder massage. I began requesting the pain medication.

I also had lost a lot of weight. I told people later I was 140 pounds (and 5' 6") when I started and 133 pounds when I was rescued. But that's probably not quite accurate. I was 133 pounds after about 24 hours of aggressive rehydration, one liquid meal and one huge breakfast. So I probably was closer to 130 pounds or less when I was rescued. (I like to think I wouldn't have dehydrated if I hadn't lost the water bottle in Boulder Creek.)

But I knew from my 3-hour training runs on the YMCA treadmill where I would lose five to six pounds that it would come back pretty quickly. I regained almost seven pounds by the Saturday afternoon I was released from the hospital. I got another two pounds back in about a week.

Yet despite my numerous injuries the two things that had my doctor so concerned and kept me in the hospital were the blisters on my heels — and my bloodwork.

My heels were sooo bad, my doctor had a "wound specialist," registered nurse Lynda Minor, visit me to examine them and change the bandages. Brenda told me that John Brewer stopped by when those bandages on my heels were being changed. He was rather taken aback. It was the first indication he had that I wasn't "fine." I ended up changing the bandages on my heels and Band-Aids on my shins daily and wearing slippers for three weeks after being released.

I also kept having an orderly come to my room a couple of times a day to draw blood for lab tests. I didn't know what the term "CPK," or creatine phosphokinase, meant that was used in charts. So I looked it up. "CPK is an enzyme found predominantly in the heart, brain, and skeletal muscle. When the total CPK level is substantially elevated, it usually indicates injury or stress to one or more of these areas."

The normal range for this enzyme in a person's blood is 35-232. Following my first blood test, mine was at 5,431. Later I was asking the hospital nutritionist if I should increase the protein in my diet to rebuild the muscle I thought I had lost. She said no, just continue with a regular diet. Then she added that I was lucky I didn't go into kidney failure. I began to get an idea of just what I had been through and how I could have ended up, even if rescued.

Dr. Oakes had floated the idea of possibly discharging me on Friday afternoon but my wounded heels and crazy bloodwork kept me there a third night.

I hadn't been hospitalized since my last brain surgery in late September 1992. When I had that deviated septum surgery in January 2001, it was as an outpatient. Afterwards, I went back to my parents' house in Bellevue and literally watched television for a week. But I had breaks for meals and they had cable television. I had forgotten how monotonous 18 hours of television can become, cable or not.

I had made a deal with the nurse that if I continued drinking fluids, she would disconnect the IV tube. So fortunately, I was able to break up my routine somewhat, not just with the numerous phone calls and visits but also with that ancient ritual of hospital recovery — walking laps around the hospital wing.

CHAPTER 21

Brenda and Chris picked me up from the hospital on Saturday afternoon. I had to wear the hospital pajamas home because the clothes recovered from my car had been stuffed in a bag with my wet clothes from the emergency room for three days.

I was in such a hurry to get out I left before my IV was removed. The nurse had asked if it had been removed and I said yes. But it only had been disconnected. The IV tubing remained stuck in my arm, clamped off. I noticed it when we got back to my apartment and I began changing out of the hospital pajamas. "Brenda? We have to go back to the hospital."

After the return trip to the hospital, we went into the newspaper office. I checked and mostly cleaned out my e-mail. I also collected my winnings from the previous week's office football pool and filled out the next week's. Lost in the wilderness for three days but I still didn't miss a week of the pool. I missed winning the overall season by two points. Two points!

Brenda told me that Henry, one of the ones who told people I was fine, was surprised to see me hunched over and walking slowly when I came in Saturday. People also asked Brenda later why she was buying me cans of protein drink. "Didn't you see how skinny he is?," she replied.

My family had gone grocery shopping for me but left the bags at my desk instead of in the refrigerator. So the quart of yogurt I had counted on for lunch was inedible.

Then we went back to my apartment again. Brenda said she and Chris would go to the store and get me several things I needed, including slippers. The bandages on my heels were too big for me to wear shoes. They said they would be back in about half an hour or so. I was hungry but didn't want to cook anything or spend the money to have a pizza delivered. So before Brenda and Chris got back, I managed to sneak out (without slippers or shoes) to Gordy's Pizza a couple of miles away. The pizza seemed too expensive and would take too long, so I got a sandwich instead. I was surprised nobody said anything to me. I got back before Chris and Brenda returned. In retrospect, I should have just had a pizza delivered.

Brenda and Chris returned and presented me with a shopping bag that had the slippers, cans of protein drink and one or two other things. Then they said they would check on me later and left.

I remember just standing there, alone, in the silence. It was an odd feeling, being back in my apartment again. I've returned from being on vacation for a week and a half and the apartment has felt sort of chilly. This was different. This had been an unexpected absence. So instead of the usual pre-vacation preparations, everything was left just as though I was coming back later that day. It was as though the aliens had decided they didn't want to kidnap me after all — "This one's no good, too skinny." — and returned me to Earth. But there also was the realization that I almost never saw this place again. As I said, it was an odd feeling.

I ventured out later to the Safeway store to buy detergent so I could make some dent in the mound of laundry I hadn't done before my disappearance. This was where I encountered Fritz C., the checker who remembered serving me the day I went missing. As I said, it was probably the weirdest part of my entire ordeal, tying the end back to the beginning.

I stayed home Sunday, spending the day watching football and trying unsuccessfully to get the knots out of my neck, shoulders and upper back. This time I decided to splurge on the pizza. The woman who delivered it turned out to be one of my karaoke groupies.

On Monday I had the first of two visits from home health nurses to change the bandages on my heels. The first nurse told me the reason there's a nursing shortage is all the paperwork they must fill out. Three hours later, she finished my paperwork and began treating my wounded heels. Three hours. I answered "No" to most of the myriad questions, too. I hate to guess how many hours it takes with those patients who answer "Yes" a lot.

The second nurse, Barbara, turned out to be John Brewer's girlfriend. They had met while John's wife Ann was dying of cancer. They became a couple with Ann's blessing. Then either the insurance company or the home health agency decided that since I actually could leave my home, I didn't qualify.

After the nurse left, I decided it was time to run some errands.

I'm fond of saying that living in a small town (or city, in this case) is like living in a benign dictatorship such as Singapore: You give up certain freedoms in exchange for security. It's a little stifling to have everyone recognize you, especially when for it's for something infamous. However, there's a certain security in having everyone you meet say they are glad you're OK and never to do that again. There's also a certain security in being able to thank your U.S. Coast Guard rescuer and several of your searchers in person.

As I ventured out Monday into a very relieved community for only the third time since my disappearance eight days earlier, I was unsure what response I would receive. I was bracing myself for a barrage of attention, although no one seemed to recognize me when I had snuck out the day before.

I fully expected something along the lines of "HEY! I recognize you! You're the guy from the newspaper! The lost hiker!" I did have a few of those. But my first two encounters were blessedly far more low-key. I went to the Safeway pharmacy to pick up a prescription I'd ordered before my hike. The woman behind the counter gave no indication she recognized me until I was paying for my prescription. I don't know if she recognized me or the name on the debit card readout, but she had his slowly spreading smile. She didn't even look up as she asked, "How are you feeling?" I said I was sore but otherwise good. I had virtually the same encounter with the clerk at the small grocery store down the street from my apartment.

I also went by Crazy Fish on Monday to let everyone know I was OK. When I got settled down in the critical care unit on Thursday, I thought about calling, then I decided that was going a little overboard. Based upon the welcome back I received, I should have called. (I didn't even know at that time about everything that had happened there the Tuesday I was missing or about the newspaper staff calling them first.) I tried opening the door but it was locked. I was walking away when the bartender Dara leaned out the door and yelled to me. Everyone was very glad to see me. It turned out they were having a crew meeting. I came in and saw the entire crew there getting the "always ask for identification" spiel from the state liquor board agent. I didn't realize how many people I'd seen there regularly were employees.

I also finally got my jeans back from the park service on Monday, but not before getting, scolded would be the polite term, by Chief Ranger Tim Simonds.

I had left messages with Ranger Titus to arrange picking up my jeans that had been used to give Jasmine my scent to follow. I even said that I was holding his flashlight hostage and was willing to discuss a trade. I received a call back from Ranger Ericks. She invited me to come to the Olympic National Park office where she worked. She showed me the room where the search was coordinated plus digital photos taken from the search helicopter. I could see the "blue tarp" that Ranger Klanke said he saw that turned out to me.

Then she said Chief Ranger Simonds wanted to talk to me. As we were walking down to see him, it struck me that this wasn't going to be a social visit. After starting off casual and somewhat friendly, he told me about the dangers inherent in helicopter searches. His tone and volume became steadily harsher and louder. A veteran park ranger who consulted on my search, Jack Hughes, walks with a metal rod in his back from when he was in a search helicopter that crashed, Simonds said. They almost didn't see me, he said. We want people to enjoy the park wilderness but what I did put others at risk as well as myself, he concluded. As Ranger Ericks and I left the office, I got the impression the visit was not her idea.

CHAPTER 22

I've learned since talking with other people who have hydrocephalus that it tends to raise your pain threshold beyond that of the general population. I guess periodically having the lining of your brain swell against your skull and then waking up from surgery with a huge scar on your half-shaved head tends to do that.

The treatment for hydrocephalus is having Teflon tubing called a shunt surgically implanted in your brain, snaking down your neck to either your heart or, in my case, abdomen. It relieves the pressure on your brain caused by the excess spinal fluid (hence the term, "water on the brain" or "fluid on the brain"). This tubing needs replaced every few years.

The procedure involves cutting a flap in the scalp and drilling a small hole in the skull. Then a small catheter (the shunt) is passed into a ventricle of the brain. A pump (which controls the flow of excess fluid) is attached to the catheter to keep the fluid away from the brain. Another catheter is attached to the pump and tunneled under the skin, behind the ear, down the neck and chest and into the abdominal cavity.

I had these "shunt revisions" — I guess you could call them "brain surgery" — nine times in 14 years between December 1978 and October 1992 and thankfully none since.

I always recovered fairly quickly, getting released from the hospital after about three or four days. Then I would get the stitches out 7-10 days later. The exception was my last four surgeries between May and September of 1992.

I had been airlifted from Pullman Memorial Hospital to Spokane's Sacred Heart Hospital on May 17, 1992 for emergency surgery and was released May 20. Then on June 3 I caught a ride to Sacred Heart with a co-worker for another surgery. I was released on June 6. My neurosurgeon, Dr. Dean Martz, told me that he had replaced the top half of the tubing, the part that went from my brain to my collarbone. But the bottom half, from my collarbone to my abdomen, was 20 years old and eventually would need to be replaced, he said. Eventually was six weeks later, when I drove myself to Sacred Heart on July 16 for my third brain surgery in three months. It was performed on July 16 and I was released July 20. I had the stitches removed about two weeks later but the incision hadn't healed because of all the scar tissue from my numerous previous surgeries.

After a visit to the emergency room and waiting a day, I was hospitalized again. I spent the next nine days from Aug. 5-13 getting one IV drug every four hours and another every eight hours. The IV had to be changed every 18 hours or so when my veins began becoming red and hard.

Then the doctor sent me home with oral antibiotics to see if the incision would finish healing. I had a home health nurse clean the incision and put a new bandage on twice a day — for the next seven weeks. Once a week on Thursday I would make the 160-mile roundtrip from Pullman to Spokane to have Dr. Martz check if the incision was healing. Finally at the end of September, he decided to operate again to move the tubing a few inches so the previous surgical incision would heal. After my fourth surgery in five months, I was released on Sept. 30, 1992. I had the stitches removed on Oct. 8 — we have cake at work every year to celebrate — and my last doctor's visit was Oct. 22, 1992.

My recovery from the three days and nights I spent in Boulder Creek was at least as frustrating as that experience, if not more so. Those repeated surgeries, hospital and emergency room visits, doctor visits, dressing changes and 160-mile roadtrips didn't wake me up at night or make walking, typing or carrying even moderately heavy objects difficult.

My pain threshold was tested along with my patience and endurance as the knots in my neck, shoulders, back and arms lingered for two months, including through my vacation and first post-rescue half marathon. The blisters on my heels, cuts and scrapes on my shins and slivers in my hands also took their time going away.

I wore the slippers that Brenda and Chris bought me since the bandages on my feet were too big to put on shoes. I also needed something without heels to allow my heels to get better. I found it is very difficult to walk up stairs, or with any kind of speed, in footwear without heels. It was pure luck that my blisters healed well enough to wear shoes just as the rains started. The bandages on my heels and shins also had to be changed at least once a day and the blisters and cuts on my heels and shins cleaned. I still had slivers in my hands, some of which Dr. Oakes had to remove.

Probably the most debilitating side effect was I couldn't sleep well because of the tightness and soreness in my back, neck, arms and shoulders. I don't know the physiology involved but all the knots in my back caused me to lose feeling in half of my right foot for several days. Until all the soreness and stiffness finally went away, it was not unusual to wake up somewhere between 2 a.m. and 6 a.m. I would sit in the bathtub with ice cold water covering my legs, teeth chattering, and submerge my forearms until my muscles were relaxed or numbed enough that I could go back to sleep.

Then I would wake up in the late morning, an hour or two later than usual. I would put on my loose brown sweater over a T-shirt and ankle socks over my bandages. Then I would step into my slippers, grab my bag of medications and shuffle out the door to work.

I never could figure out if I needed ice packs or a heating pad. I often used both, keeping a heating pad plugged into the wall to help me fall asleep the first time (before being awakened in the early morning).

At first the only relief I experienced was from attending yoga classes at the Clallam County Family YMCA. (The instructor Brooke was a Crazy Fish regular at the time. She had been there the night my disappearance was announced.) Many of the poses were beyond the capabilities of my still sore upper torso, so I spent a lot of time in the resting pose. It still helped to relax my back, neck and shoulders, though. Brooke told me later she didn't realize I was injured, she just thought I was bored.

Just as I had done with the pain medication in the hospital, I declined when offered a prescription for pain killers. "He really doesn't think he needs to have an oral narcotic analgesic," Dr. Oakes wrote in his report. I wasn't being macho. I didn't think it would be necessary. I was wrong.

I had numerous packets of extra strength pain medications from my races over the years. You get all those kinds of things in "goody bags" along with your race T-shirt either before or after the race. Most of this stuff gets thrown in a drawer and forgotten. I quickly went through my stash I had accumulated over the years and had to buy more. I eventually found that one of those 22-ounce beers that cost about a buck and a half was at least as effective, if not more.

Writing on a notepad and typing all day probably didn't help my recovery given the muscles used. I covered a long night meeting on Wednesday, September 21, only my second day back. I also ended up working that Sunday for Jim Casey, who had filled in for me that Friday I was in the hospital. I worked 10 of the next 11 days after returning to work.

My recovery probably also was not helped by grabbing that large bottle of detergent off a high shelf at the Safeway store and then carrying it around the store. Especially since it was only two days after getting out of the hospital. That probably added another couple of weeks to my recovery right there.

All this soreness did have the benefit of introducing me to the wonders of professional massage. Professional massage is a far cry from the places that advertise they are open 24 hours a day and take MasterCard, Visa and Discover. I wasn't sure if

I needed a masseuse (apparently they prefer the term "licensed massage practitioner") or a chiropractor. I visited Dr. Oakes again who told me it was just muscle soreness and gave me a referral for massage. I wasn't able to get to my first massage until Monday afternoon, more than a week after getting released from the hospital on Saturday.

I went to Mindy's Massage over in Carlsborg between Port Angeles and Sequim. This is where I met Merry, a friendly young mother of two boys from Alaska. She had been practicing massage for five years. People laugh when I say this but she had GREAT elbows. She would use them to grind the knots out of my back and shoulders. It was an amazing feeling afterwards, as though I had just finished a workout.

The most debilitating of the knots was right between my shoulder blades, just below my neck. As I was sitting at my desk at work on Tuesday evening a day after my first massage, I suddenly felt it disappear. I was hooked on professional massage, especially Merry and those elbows.

I went again on Saturday and then about once a week for the next two months. It was the morning of Nov. 17, exactly two months after getting out of the hospital when I felt slipknot in the muscles of my right arm slide undone. I don't know how long it was until I could look over my shoulder — either one — at City Council meetings but I was cured, at least physically. Now I only visit Merry for post-marathon recovery.

I sent thank you cards to both Merry and my yoga instructor.

CHAPTER 23

I've discovered since my karaoke singing has brought me
unexpected notoriety, including groupies in three states
(Washington plus Nevada and Arizona where I vacation),
that I'm a rather private person. It took me a long time to adjust
to the attention that my singing brought me, including the
post-performance congratulations, compliments and even song
requests. (Plus the random calls of "Brian G!" from groupies
as I was spotted in Port Angeles, or in the bathroom of the
ferry between Bainbridge Island and Seattle.) Fortunately, that
background provided good training as I began to be welcomed
back by large groups of people who knew me versus just random
individuals.

Dr. Oakes said I could return to work on Wednesday but I
was determined to come back sooner. I'm not sure why I was so
eager to return to what can be a high stress job except the strong
desire to get back to normal.

When I returned to work on Tuesday, I walked through
the door in the late morning, hunched over with my back, neck
and shoulder pain. I was spotted by two women in the circulation
department. They both looked at me with an endearing "Awww"
expression.

After I had been at work for a couple of hours, everyone
(except Brenda, who was at another job) gathered around and
presented me with a Welcome Back card and a backpack. Brenda

told me that when my co-workers heard I was OK, they were going to send me flowers. Then they decided to give me things I could actually use. So they passed the hat and went to Swains, the local outdoors and general store whose motto is "We have everything."

The backpack I received contained just about everything — matches, map, poncho, multi-tool, water bottle, compass — all individually wrapped too. Several of those items would have come in very handy during my ordeal, which I guess was the idea.

I also received similar items from my sister, landlord, stepbrother and apartment house owners. Of course, I ended up with two of some things and three compasses. On future hikes I brought all this stuff, in sharp contrast to my prior "psycho hikes." After getting all those gifts, I decided that regardless of obvious reasons for bringing all these things, to do otherwise would be, well, rude.

Henry took numerous digital photographs of the gift presentation that he then posted on a Yahoo! page.

I also was welcomed back at meetings of the Port Angeles Chamber of Commerce, Port Angeles Business Association and Port of Port Angeles, all of which I covered for the newspaper. But not the Port Angeles Planning Commission, which was a little odd. It began to get a little embarrassing. As I said, my karaoke experience helped greatly here. Such as when I was asked to lead the Pledge of Allegiance at the PABA meeting. That was weird. I don't even participate in the pledge, conveniently ducking out beforehand. It is probably a result of going to elementary school in the 1970s. But I've come to associate the ritual with countries we like to ridicule. So it was weird leading the pledge.

Perhaps the most surprising welcome back was at the Clallam County Family YMCA. When I scanned my automated entry card, a welcome back message appeared on the computer screen along with my registration information.

Undoubtedly the most embarrassing welcome back I received was when I received the proclamation from the Port Angeles City Council at its Sept. 20 meeting. Fortunately, I was shuffling across the street to the Clallam County Courthouse to drop off my primary election ballot. So I missed getting my photograph in my own newspaper, again.

Mayor Richard Headrick presented the proclamation to me later in the meeting, after our newspaper's photographer had left. It read:

"Brian Gawley is well-known in the City of Port Angeles for his steadfast coverage of the news and events of the City Council meetings of Port Angeles.

Brian is also known for his love of marathon running, and Brian loves to train for these many events by entering the backcountry and getting a workout to prepare for a marathon; and on Sunday, September 11, 2005, Brian chose to use the area around Olympic Hot Springs to get a high-altitude workout, but didn't share this information with his fellow associates and friends at work;

and Brian began his journey by running along the trail and then decided to see what was on the other side of the mountain, or see where another trail lead;

and as nightfall approached, he had not made it back to the starting point of the trailhead and became the equivalent of lost in the mountains;

and over the three days plus, as Brian was enjoying the great outdoors, he stumbled and fell several times, bumping his head, which led to losing his glasses, which really made it harder to find his way;

and Brian realized he had actually now used up several vacation days, since he didn't return to work on Monday. So, hungry, tired, limping, and determined, Brian kept up his dogged walk with unwavering belief that he would survive to tell his tale;

and Brian was blessed with great friends at work who made the effort to find his car, alert the authorities, file a missing person report and organize the Park Service and Coast Guard to go out and get Brian,

Now, therefore, the City Council of Port Angeles urges all Brian's friends to be thankful for his somewhat safe return and join the Council in asking Brian to PLEASE TELL SOMEONE WHERE HE IS GOING, carry an extra pair of glasses, a survival pack, maybe a GPS, and find a training buddy to be with for his next great adventure.

Brian we are all so glad you were determined to come back to cover the City Council's exciting news stories! That is dedication! Happy Trails to You.

Richard Headrick September 20, 2005"

The presentation was supposed to be followed by a recording of "Happy Trails" but they experienced "technical difficulties."

People's recognition of me wasn't always immediate. I had several people ask, "You were the one in the newspaper, right?" or questions to that effect. It did linger though, at least the story. Months later I would tell the story and the person would ask, "That was you?" My notoriety did save me time in identifying myself on a couple of occasions. One was when the home health agency called to set up my appointment, the woman said, "This doesn't say what kind of surgery you've had."

"I'm the one the Coast Guard hoisted out of the park."

"Oh, yeah."

The most amusing encounter was with Julie at the annual Christmas party. She had worked in the newspaper's circulation department at a desk literally on the other side of the office partition from me. She always would say the most amusing things to either co-workers or callers that would send me around the partition to announce, "That one is going on your 'Greatest Hits' tape." Then she moved to the Seattle area briefly, returning obviously after my rescue.

We began talking and she asked, "So, what's been happening with you? What have you been doing? What's been going on?"

But just as I was taught in the Edward R. Murrow Department of Communications at Washington State University in the late 1980s, the public can have a short memory.

One of my all-time favorite movies is "This Is Spinal Tap," a wickedly biting satire of the rise, fall and rise again of a British heavy metal rock band. One of my favorite scenes is when the band is making its comeback from obscurity. They have managed to get booked at a county fair. They used to perform before thousands of adoring fans in football stadiums. Now they are playing the county fair. Adding insult to injury, the reader board advertises "Puppet Show and Spinal Tap." The band's new manager, Jeanine Pettibone, protests, "I've told them a hundred times: put Spinal Tap first and Puppet Show last."

As much as I was beginning to enjoy the return of my relative anonymity, I engaged in that same desperate grasping for fading celebrity as my ordeal began fading into the past.

A co-worker from our Port Townsend office called and I told him the part of the story about falling and breaking my glasses. After I hung up, my editor Dean said the newsroom was tired of hearing the same story over and over and to go into another room next time. I just replied that their jealousy was so obviously transparent.

Another indication of my fading celebrity was when one of the Safeway checkers, Donna, asked me how I was feeling. "Much better, thanks," I said. "Oh, have you been feeling bad lately?," she replied, innocently. I was aghast. I said, "I was the one who got airlifted out of the park." I'm not sure that jogged her memory.

I began to realize the readerboard now proclaimed "Puppet Show" then "Lost Hiker Returns." It wasn't entirely a bad thing.

CHAPTER 24

My return to Crazy Fish later that Tuesday night after the City Council meeting was nothing short of remarkable - and humbling. The karaoke show started about 9 p.m. but I didn't arrive until about 10:30 p.m. because of the meeting.

I didn't expect and wasn't prepared for the response I received upon returning to my Tuesday night hangout.

(After I had said in the newspaper I would be singing there that night the co-owner Cypress Vollmer said, "Thanks for the plug." But I expected THAT.)

Unfortunately, I couldn't drink that night. I was less than a week removed from a nutritionist telling me I almost had gone into renal failure. I didn't think drinking would be a good idea.

As I was standing in the rather slow-moving drink line to get a diet Coke, people kept telling me they were glad I was found. The 20-something crowd there isn't exactly part of newspapers' shrinking demographic. So I didn't know if they had seen my story on the local cable television newscast or Seattle newscasts, heard it on the radio or read it in the newspaper. Of course, in small towns, or cities, that kind of news travels pretty quickly by word of mouth.

I didn't know what had gone on there the week before. Apparently Cypress called the newspaper to ask why I wasn't there the Tuesday I was missing. The nightclub also was one of the newspaper staff's first calls after getting word of my rescue. When she heard the news, Cypress exclaimed that they were going to throw the biggest party upon my return the next Tuesday.

She wasn't far off in her declaration.

Andy called me at home on Saturday for a Sunday story about my release from the hospital. When I told him I planned to sing at Crazy Fish on Tuesday, he asked what song I was going to sing. I replied "Someone Saved My Life Tonight." It is one of the few cliché things I said during this whole experience.

The song really isn't about what the title might suggest. It's about a guy who is glad he escaped from a relationship from hell. But it still sends chills through me when I hear the lines, "You almost had your hooks in me, didn't you dear? You nearly had me roped and tied."

I KNEW what song I was going to sing. EVERYBODY knew what song I was going to sing. It was the song I HAD to sing. Queen's Bohemian Rhapsody had become my signature song since I first performed it in October 1999 at Michael's On The Lake in Moses Lake. It was only the second song I had ever performed in public.

I also had a strong emotional connection to it. The song was released on Halloween 1975 and received most of its airplay during the summer of 1976, which was when my mother was dying of leukemia. I can remember listening to it over and over on my first real record player. But as the fall approached and my mother still was in the hospital, I stopped listening to the song because of its references to mothers and death. I relented some months later, although I don't remember when.

I've reached the point in my performing career, karaoke anyway, where I can scan the crowd while I'm singing. It depends upon the song, of course, but often the music is background. I'm doing a cover version, after all. This was different. I had what seemed like everyone in the bar standing in front of the stage. They were watching me with that same kind of "Awwwww" look I received from the two women when I returned to work earlier that day.

As the first strains of Queen's frenetic rock opera wafted across the crowd, I got goosebumps.

"Is this the real life? Is this just fantasy?
Caught in a landslide, no escape from reality.
Open your eyes, look up to the sky and see.
I'm just a poor boy, I need no sympathy
Because I'm easy come, easy go
Little high, little low
Anyway the wind blows
Doesn't really matter to me
To me"

After the first verse, I settled down and it became just another performance. It actually turned out to be one of my best performances of a difficult song. Then came what always has been the more difficult part for me — when the music ends and I walk off the stage to the applause, high fives and other congratulations. I don't know if it was easier or more difficult that night.

I sang once or twice more and also helped someone with a Led Zeppelin song. I can remember people coming up behind me and putting their hands on my shoulders and back and congratulating me. Those hands felt GREAT given all the knots in my back, neck and shoulders. Two of my searchers were there that night. I also had one person tell me that he took my X-rays.

Katrina spent much of the night teaching me how to dance. It bore an eerie resemblance to some of my least favorite voice lessons. One-two-three. One-two-three. One-two-three. I also was called up behind the bar to get my picture taken with Cypress and Dara. Cypress put a hat on me. It was one of those paper birthday hats with the string that goes under your chin. It wasn't until the next day that a co-worker pointed out to me the condom stuck in the top of it.

I had my picture taken showing Cypress and Dara with an arm each around my shoulders. Cypress took three other photos, but wouldn't give me that one. She said it was going up on the nightclub's Web site. I never did see it and she said later no one could find it.

The next Tuesday, one of the employees gave me a hat and said Cypress wanted me to have it. It was almost identical to the one I usually wore but a little smaller. Cypress liked hats. She sometimes would make all the nightclub employees wear one during crew meetings. She had just bought this one but thought I looked so sad with no hat and a bandage on my forehead that Tuesday that she gave it to me.

A couple of weeks later, she also gave me a bottle of the wine that I usually drank on Tuesday nights. I refer to it as my $13,500 bottle of wine. It's not because it would sell for that much. It's because it only required a $10,000 search and rescue, a $2,000 hospital stay (my portion of it) and $1,500 in doctor, dentist and massage bills (my portion, again) to get.

Everyone was in such a good mood the night I returned, in sharp contrast to the previous week, that they sang and danced all night. The staff finally had to turn on the lights and announce that it was five minutes past when we could legally be in the place and everyone had to leave NOW!

I shuffled off down the street to my car at the newspaper office wearing my sweater, my slippers and the birthday hat Cypress had put on me, carrying my three photographs. It was 2:15 a.m. I may not have looked the part but I was perfectly sober.

CHAPTER 25

I already was signed up for what had become my annual October trip to Lake Tahoe, Reno and northern Nevada. Since 2002, I would visit Lake Tahoe, Reno and northern Nevada in October, then Las Vegas, southern Nevada and Flagstaff, Arizona in March. (I would stay in Flagstaff and visit both the Grand Canyon and spring training baseball in the Phoenix area.)

But as I wasn't over my injuries yet, carrying my duffel bags — one large and one medium-sized — presented a problem. I would carry them for a while, set them down, roll my shoulders, switch the larger one to the other arm and continue walking. It was one of the few times I paid the $3 for one of those luggage carts. I also kept one of my duffel bags in the rental car for a couple of days before lugging it up to my hotel room.

The tenth annual Lake Tahoe Marathon and Half Marathon was held on Saturday, Oct. 8, 2005, 24 days after my rescue and three weeks after being released from the hospital.

When I first ran the Lake Tahoe Marathon in October 2002, I responded to an ad for Twin Peaks Chalet located just outside the race's starting point of Tahoe City. It was operated by Dave and Brenda Giese, who were both hard-core recreationists. Brenda has hiked the Grand Canyon from the rim to the river and back in one day, which those full-page, four-color advertisements advise you against. They have numerous photographs around the house of all their hiking, skiing and other adventures. The next year they continued to operate the chalet but didn't advertise. Now they just operate it for friends, of which I was considered one.

I did the half marathon — walking. I ran the final 2.1 miles in an unsuccessful effort to finish in less than three hours. I found the running helped loosen up some of the now three-week-old muscle stiffness in my upper back and shoulders. I finished in 3:03:15, a pace of 13:59 a mile or a little faster than four miles an hour. I thought later I should have mentioned to the race director that 24 days earlier I had been in intensive care after three unprepared days and nights in the wilderness. But maybe that would have been too much self-promotion.

After I left the Gieses, I drove over to the Sands Regency in Reno where I had really cheap room rates. My vacations to the Southwest usually are a whirlwind. "If it's Tuesday, this must be Death Valley," as I put it. But as my injuries prevented me from getting a full night's sleep, this one was a lot more subdued. I would wake up, put on my brown sweater and slippers, and shuffle downstairs to the casino. Usually I would have gone to a nearby casino for the breakfast buffet. This time I bought the breakfast sandwich and coffee special from the casino's coffee shop. Then I would play "The Munsters" penny slot machine for most of the day. It was very relaxing.

I also hit one of my mainstays of these trips, karaoke at the Second Street Bar in downtown Reno. Walking around that place with a cordless microphone singing Billy Joel's "Piano Man" is an experience to remember. For my last song of the trip, I did Elton John's "Someone Saved My Life Tonight," dedicated to the U.S. Coast Guard. Nobody there could fully appreciate it, of course.

I kept having to remind myself that although I didn't do a lot of the usual vacation activities, the trip still was beneficial for the relaxation. I also kept reminding myself that I was about a month removed from spending three days and nights in a backcountry creek in running shorts with no food.

I did get to hike the Mount Rose Trail, a 12-mile round-trip to 10,776 feet, which was quite an experience. The trailhead is located about 30 miles south of Reno, just off the Mount Rose

Highway. I took my new backpack and headed out in the mid-morning. The trail starts at about 7,000 feet and climbs to the 10,776-foot summit within its six miles.

I made it to the top in good time, which was an incredible experience both for the thin air as well as the spectacular vistas. Then I had to get back to down, though. This was where I had, um, trouble last time.

So I latched onto this older gentleman who was training for a hike in South America or Colorado somewhere. I say latched onto because I felt this almost-pathological need to stick with him, even if his pace was slower than mine. He did point out the three California reservoirs that are supposed to be visible from the trail high in Nevada. He stopped once with the expectation (or hope) that I would keep going. When he stopped a second time, I either took the hint or wanted to get to the trailhead as soon as possible. So I left him behind and continued down the trail.

I encountered two separate pairs of 20-something males without backpacks or water bottles, which was OK because we all know they'll live forever. I also encountered a father and his young son similarly unequipped. I thought about turning around and scolding both of them but didn't. I also encountered, I swear, a very well-conditioned runner, by himself, wearing nothing but running shorts. That's it.

I had begun in plenty of time to make it back down before sundown but that is thinking rationally. I was three and a half weeks removed from a near-death experience on a high country trail such as this one. I was far more emotional than rational. As I neared the bottom I asked two people who were just starting up the trail how much further I had to go. One of them told me about 40 minutes. I could have sworn I was 20 minutes from the bottom. (There's that infamous 20 minutes from the bottom again.) As I continued down the trail I began to think he was trying to mess with my head. After 20 minutes passed and there was no trailhead in sight, I began to get...anxious. As I saw other people coming up the trail though, including the runner, I began to calm down. I finally reached the trailhead safely in daylight.

But the more hair-raising experience was when I visited the Black Rock Desert about 100 miles north of Reno on my vacation's last day. Besides being where land speed records are set, it's best known for the Burning Man Festival held in late August. But that's only once a year at a time I don't go, costs a fortune, and takes more time than I can afford to devote during these vacations. I went to the Black Rock Desert for the experience of visiting one of the flattest, most desolate places on Earth. Death Valley is great too, but it gets a lot more visitors. I stopped at a gas station in Nixon or Gerlach to get gas for the rental car. I had rented the car with a full tank of gas. I was supposed to return it empty. Anything left in the tank would be lost. So I told the guy to give me only four or five gallons. I figured that would get me to where I was going and back to here (or another gas station), where I could get enough gas to get back to Reno. I didn't have the time or daylight to drive much further than the distance four or five gallons would carry me anyway.

I drove up the highway until I found somewhere that looked like a good place to stop. Then I walked out onto the flat high desert playa. I didn't drive out onto it because I had read that if you hit a wet spot on this flat desert sand, you'd be hopelessly stuck. I went out further and further, watching my shadow get longer and longer. Fortunately, getting lost wasn't an issue. I just needed to walk back towards the mountains towering behind the highway. The worst case scenario would have been ending up a ways down the highway from my car. Dehydration also was not an issue, since it was the late afternoon in northern Nevada in mid-October. A shortage of tissues turned out to be the bigger concern. Getting back to Reno turned out to be the biggest concern, though.

I began to watch the gas gauge closely as it seemed to be dropping more steadily than the number of miles back to Reno on the highway signs. I can't remember if the first town I reached, Nixon, either didn't have a gas station or didn't have one that was open. All I remember is looking for somewhere, anywhere, to buy gas before Reno in the seventh largest state in the country.

I remember keeping up a steady, moderate (for that area) speed and coasting wherever possible to maximize gas mileage. I think I ended up stopping in Wadsworth, several miles to the south. You'd be surprised how bright that gas gauge light can be or how loud it can be when it lights up.

CHAPTER 26

My sister asked me shortly after my release from the hospital if I had suffered from post-traumatic stress disorder. (I guess now it's called post-traumatic stress syndrome, removing the stigma of a "disorder.") I said no at the time but there's actually been several situations since that probably would qualify to some extent.

The therapist told me that you always will have some negative reaction to places and events connected with an experience like this, although they usually become less intense over time. The key, he said, is how you deal with them.

I explained that to people later this way, "The key is not shooting up a small Oregon town." (I would add the reference to Sylvester Stallone's 1982 movie "First Blood" just in case they didn't get it.)

In the months following my rescue, I was amazed at the variety of "triggers" that would suddenly bring back the feelings from those days and nights in the creek.

I happened to be watching television one Friday evening after returning from vacation when I saw a promo for the Discovery Channel series, "I Shouldn't Be Alive." Of course, I felt compelled to watch, especially since I still wasn't completely over my injuries.

The second episode of the first season, "Lost in the Snow," aired Nov. 4. It concerned a U.S. Army private, his wife and their four-month-old son who were driving from central California to a funeral in Idaho. The main highway was closed by a blizzard. So they took a detour, missed a snow-covered "Road Closed" sign and became stranded in the Sheldon National Wildlife Refuge in northwestern Nevada.

They were miles from anywhere with nothing but snow as far as the eye could see. After staying with their truck for five days, they began hiking to find the highway -- in the wrong direction. Finally, the husband left his wife and baby in a cave and hiked back the way they had come. He eventually reached the highway. He was spotted by a passing car and his family was rescued.

I was spellbound.

They drove into a snowstorm without chains. They missed an important sign and ended up hopelessly lost. They went one direction, decided it was a dead end and headed back the way they had come. They stay put for a while, then decide to try finding help.

They had told people where they were going but took a detour so no one would have known where to look for them. The husband was hallucinating as he hiked miles and miles with no food and only snow for water.

I found myself watching in morbid fascination and empathy. I kept saying to myself, "Yeah, that happened to me." "I used that reasoning." "I began feeling that way."

I watched the "Escape from the Amazon" episode the next Friday, Nov. 11, with similar reactions. I've seen several other episodes since with varying degrees of morbid fascination depending on the circumstances.

I also read "Between A Rock And A Hard Place" by Aron Ralston. He is the hardcore mountain climber and outdoorsman who had his right forearm trapped by a boulder in Utah's Canyonlands National Park. He was trapped from mid-day April 26, 2003 until mid-day May 1, 2003 — six days and five nights. The part everyone remembers and focuses on is the self-amputation of his right forearm, but there's so much more to his story and to the book.

He survived all that time with only two burritos to eat and only urine to drink after the first couple of days. He survived the loneliness and isolation, the cold and the hallucinations. He was rescued despite not telling anyone explicitly where he was going or when he would return. Once again, I absorbed it all with morbid fascination and empathy. I finished all 368 pages in about a week.

Some of the most severe "flashbacks" — if you want to use that term — were connected with Billy Joel's "You May Be Right."

It was playing on the public address system in the Safeway store sometime after I got out of the hospital. I almost went running out of the store. I really should have. The next time that happened, I did.

Then in April 2006, about seven months after my rescue, it happened again.

I was at Crazy Fish on a Tuesday when someone got up to sing karaoke and a familiar tune and lyrics began to penetrate my brain. When I realized it was "You May Be Right," I grabbed my coat (it was still early spring in the 48th Parallel) and went running across the nightclub. I ran out the door and down the street far enough that I couldn't hear the song coming out of the doorway. I squatted there in the middle of the street and collected myself until I figured the song was over.

The deejay was Dan Erwin. Paul and I had been over at his house that Saturday night before my hike. So he was familiar with my experience. He told me later that although I was next up to sing, he skipped to the next singer. Something obviously was wrong and he pretty much knew or suspected what it was. (When I related the experience to my father he said that maybe I should consider seeing a therapist.)

I had vowed that I was never going to perform that song again anywhere. Ever. But my therapist explained that I would have to if I wanted to overcome my experience. I've done it once or twice since then, including to mark the one-year anniversary of my rescue.

The Port Angeles Chamber of Commerce normally holds its Monday noon luncheon meetings at the Red Lion Hotel. The first one I covered after getting back to work though was held at the Port Angeles Yacht Club. I still cover the luncheon meetings when they are held there, but I don't like it.

I can still listen to Elton John's "Someone Saved My Life Tonight." It's not really about what the title might suggest. It's about a guy who is glad he escaped from a relationship from hell. But it still sends chills through me when I hear the lines, "You almost had your hooks in me, didn't you dear? You nearly had me roped and tied."

When I was visiting my family at Christmas, I was showing my father photographs I had taken during the hike. The final one showed Klahhane Ridge between the trees with a backdrop of clouds. It was almost the exact scene I saw that Wednesday afternoon when I first noticed the clouds. I shook off the chilling feeling that overcame me and put the photographs away.

It wasn't just television or music or photographs that could do it, though.

About two and a half months after my rescue, I was driving to the ferry landing after spending Thanksgiving with my family in Bellevue. I was trying to catch the next ferry back to the Olympic Peninsula from Seattle, which is about 10 or so miles away from Bellevue across Lake Washington. The early evening sun also was setting. Suddenly I had the same kind of anxious feeling I had trying to reach the asphalt section of the Appleton Pass Trail before sundown.

It wasn't the only time I found myself getting anxious in the early morning or late evening. I usually don't wake up early enough to see sunrises. Those mornings in the creek were one of the times I that did manage to see the sunrise.

Probably the most intense sensations though, and the ones that caught me completely off-guard, were connected to the weather and the calendar.

In mid-August 2006, I had to get up at 6 a.m. to interview a Washington Conservation Corps crew before they went into the forest for several days. When I stepped outside my apartment that chilly early morning air with a clear sky in the late summer felt all too familiar. I had to stop and take a couple of deep breaths before continuing to my car.

Then on the night of Sunday, Sept. 10, 2006, one year after I first went missing, I drove out to the grocery store. It was a clear night. It was dark. It was a little chilly, maybe about 50 degrees. It was the second week of September, albeit a year later. It was as close as I've ever come to hyperventilating.

As I was getting out of bed one day many weeks after my rescue, I noticed the heating pad still plugged into the wall. I don't know how long it had been that way. I unplugged it, but left it there. I don't think it was laziness or bad housekeeping, or even convenience. I think it was wanting to leave myself a reminder of what I endured for the two months after getting out of the hospital. You would think no reminder would be necessary but as we go about our daily lives, those things can get lost. That heating pad is still there, unplugged, between my bed and the wall.

For a while afterwards, I would put my name into Google and read the entries that came up. I've written so many of those newspaper articles during my 11 years as a newspaper reporter that to be reading about myself was surreal.

I would read the park service releases, PDN stories and Seattle TV station stories. I even found a Web site called AngelsMissing. com that catalogued these stories. I would say to myself, "That was me! %&%*%$#%, I was pulled out of a *&^*^&* backcountry creek by a $^&%$#%# Coast Guard helicopter."

Months afterwards, it still sends shivers through me to read:

"A search began yesterday afternoon for 39-year old Brian Gawley of Port Angeles, who is overdue from a planned day hike on Sunday. Field searchers and a bloodhound team are continuing the search today, with a helicopter to join the effort this afternoon."

It's the kind of thing I've written dozens of times myself. But it's different when it's you. It is one reason I decided to write this book, as catharsis, before this experience became an unhealthy, fatalistic or self-destructive obsession.

I also searched our newspaper's archive of past stories that most people refer to as "the library." I use the old-timers' term "the morgue." This archive often is several weeks behind. Finally, it was caught up to the point where the stories of my disappearance, search and rescue were available. I'm sure I wasn't thinking when I announced, "Hey, I'm in the morgue!" It was one of those awkward moments that inevitably is followed by laughs of relief.

There's a chain e-mail letter that says you should appreciate things such as the leak in the roof - because it means you have a roof over your head, or annoying co-workers - because it means you have a job. I know that after almost dying a slow death alone in a harsh, remote location where my body may or may not have been recovered, I'm supposed to appreciate even the little things about being alive.

But that e-mail strikes me as a little too cliché. I don't want to cheapen my experience and the efforts of my rescuers with clichés. For example, the toilet in my apartment needed a new valve. After being flushed, it ran and ran and ran until I finally had to shut off the water. It was annoying before I was rescued. It was STILL annoying after I was rescued. It wasn't a big deal but it was annoying. (It finally was fixed.)

The experience has made me, not only more appreciative of some things, but also less patient with others. The top of the list, of course, is the television series "Survivor." Yeah, right. Give those contestants a walking stick, a watch, a water bottle, running shorts, a windshirt, a French Foreign Legion-type hat and a lot of caring people back in civilization. Then stick them in a backcountry creek for three days — without the camera crew or anyone knowing where they are or even if they are missing — and see if they "survive."

I've never had much patience with discussions of probabilities versus possibilities. Smokers are big on that one. The argument goes that the person knows someone who has smoked for years with no problems, so it must not be that big a deal. The argument focuses on the possibility of no complications while ignoring the probability of those same complications. I survived meningitis (by a matter of minutes) and have lived with hydrocephalus for almost 40 years with no serious complications. That doesn't mean everyone is going to turn out like that. It's possible, but not probable. Now I really have no patience with that discussion. Surviving something like this is possible, I'm proof of that, but not probable. I've written newspaper stories since illustrating that.

A lot also was made in the press reports (and my medical records) about my headfirst fall and losing my glasses, although not so much about my concussion. I suppose that's to be expected. As I said, I refuse to play the what if game. What if something had been protruding from that log or whatever I hit and got me in eye? What if I had hit or dislodged my shunt? What if I had pithed myself like a frog in a high school biology class? I decided I wasn't going to play that game not only because it's damn scary but because it wastes energy and accomplishes nothing. But I did fall a lot besides just my headfirst lurch. That's another one of the places where I was very lucky. Those numerous other slips and falls in the creek also could have been very injurious. They were certainly frustrating and added to my soreness. But it wasn't so much all the falls I took, or the headfirst one, that made this such an ordeal. It was being out in the elements under-dressed and over-worked for three days with the knowledge that no one knew where I was.

Perhaps I let the malfunctioning toilet get to me too much given my the gravity of my ordeal. I guess you could say the fact I still become annoyed at such seemingly trivial things is a good sign. It's not that I'm not ungrateful or unappreciative. It shows I'm not framing EVERYTHING in terms of life and death. It shows I'm moving on and resuming my life just as I resolved to do.

But I have "stopped to smell the roses" more often since my rescue. The experience also has made me quicker to shrug my shoulders at many otherwise irritating situations. Yes, getting stuck in the quick checkout line behind the couple that has ten items EACH is still irritating. But it's not life and death.

CHAPTER 27
(AND CODA)

S o that's my story. The National Park Service's final cost for the search and rescue was $9,888, not counting the volunteers. I spent $2,000 on my hospital stay (insurance picked up the other $8,000) and another $1,500 on doctor and dentist visits and massages. I didn't end up addicted to either painkillers or alcohol despite two months of muscle soreness.

Nobody knew where I was or even that I was missing for about 48 hours. Once the search began and my probable location was narrowed down, the search went rather quickly. A fourth night in the wilderness and I might have died, especially with the rainstorm that night. I probably also would have lost my mind. I would have at least spent more time in the emergency room and the hospital. I also certainly would have had lifelong conditions such as kidney damage or failure.

If I had been found.

It's a little overwhelming at times. I'm trying to remember who told me one of the most profound things I've ever heard. It was that I had had a unique experience. I had the opportunity to see how people would react if I died. It may have been Nancy Woods, the former fire district volunteer who contacted her sister the psychic.

Since my rescue I've run the half marathons at Lake Tahoe and Seattle and marathons at Port Angeles and Bellevue. At various points during the last three, I've almost broken down crying as I realize that after all this I'm able to do that again.

In the year after my rescue, two more hikers lost in Olympic National Park ended up on the same newspaper front page as me. One story had a happy ending like mine, one didn't.

The first was a 19-year-old woman, Dana Crane of Brunswick, Maine, who fell 25 feet from a crumbling cliff along one of the park's remote Pacific Ocean beaches in May 2006. She had a full pack but set it aside to hike along the cliff. She had applied for a backcountry permit to camp overnight but was hiking in a different area that day. Dana laid on the beach, with the tide coming perilously close, for three days before a park volunteer and his girlfriend just happened to run across her. She had managed to drag herself, with a spine broken in three places and a broken leg, to a more visible area on the beach. Dana had her whistle with her and said she never gave up hope. I tried unsuccessfully to contact her for an interview. The television reporter who did said she was a good interview. I sent her a get well card with my newspaper story enclosed.

The other was a 47-year-old man, Gilbert Gilman, who was the deputy director of the state's retirement system. He went hiking in the park's Staircase area in June 2006 wearing khaki shorts and a Hawaiian shirt. Searchers that included bloodhounds and scuba divers spent 10 days and 5,000 hours in an unsuccessful effort to locate him. They didn't even find his body.

As the search dragged on, at least one person (myself included) began to wonder if it was a suicide. A 57-year-old professor at Olympic College, Wendell "Wen" Harris, apparently did that in April 2006. He wasn't the subject of a search and rescue mission.

I still get scared on the last half of the return trip on any hike, even short ones. I don't run out of the nightclub or the grocery store anymore when "You May Be Right" begins playing. I actually have performed the karaoke version at a friend's house as well as at Crazy Fish. But if I'm in the car and that song comes on the radio, I change the station. Being in a public environment is one thing but being alone in the car with that playing would take more effort to get through than I'm willing to put out. Some of the scars on forehead and shins appear to be permanent, although not as prominent as I once thought. But I'm here. I'm alive.

I don't hike as often but that's as much a time issue as anything. I actually want to get back to it. Although I must admit this experience has taken some of the enjoyment out of those excursions, especially for the people I now let know of my whereabouts.

I guess I'm supposed to say this was some kind of spiritual experience. It wasn't, far from it. The entire experience was frustrating, exhausting and, near the end, terrifying. My physical recovery lasted two months, the mental and emotional even longer.

There's other clichés such as "I don't regret it. This made me what I am today." and "Whatever doesn't kill you makes you stronger." Yeah, right. I've gained a perspective that not many people have but if I could take it back I would. Whatever insights I gained about life, the universe and everything just really wasn't worth the experience.

I guess I'm also supposed to say that I've dedicated my life to charity; quit my job and joined a world relief organization or search and rescue group or something. I haven't. (Although I do take special interest in the missing hiker stories, volunteering when word of them comes into the newsroom.) I guess you could say I've decided not to dwell on my experience. I still willingly talk about it at virtually any opportunity but that is fading as I finish writing this.

I began writing the book in January 2006 after the holidays were over. I was covering the state Legislature for the newspaper, which involved a lot of sitting around waiting for the lawmakers to call me on Fridays and Saturdays. So I would write while I waited, then walk down the street to Bella Italia, a restaurant and wine bar down the street, and continue writing. This also provided an excellent, albeit expensive, avenue of promotion for the book. I suspect I also was drawn to the revival of my minor celebrity status. I would tell my story again and again to captivated people who had asked what I was writing. After awhile the wine bar staff began reacting the same way the newspaper staff did, rolling their eyes and walking away as I launched into the story again.

Then even that began to fade and the writing became just therapeutic (and enjoyable as I always had wanted to write more than just newspaper stories). It was then I began realizing that things were returning to normal.

I usually start the day with a shot (or two) of espresso in coffee. It's been called variously a piledriver, shot-in-the-dark, red-eye, sludge-cup (not my favorite) and a couple of other names. My name for it is a Lazarus, because it will raise the dead. If one of these doesn't wake you up, you probably should go back to bed.

The coffee shop in Port Angeles where I buy it is about two blocks from the newspaper office on First Street. The street isn't a particularly busy one, at least not in the late morning. But its urban setting is quite a contrast to the mountain creek where I spent three days and nights. It's also only about 20 miles north of the creek by car, 10 as the U.S. Coast Guard helicopter flies.

One day I was returning to the office from my daily caffeine pursuit when I gradually became keenly aware of my feet quietly tapping on the sidewalk. I wish I could remember the date or least the month. I slowed from my normally brisk pace. I listened to the sound of my feet, feeling them hit the pavement. I began taking in the fact I was walking down this sidewalk to work, mere miles from that creek, as though it was just another day. It was then I realized I had achieved the goal I set for myself that first night in the wilderness. I didn't just survive to be rescued.

I've got my life back.

LaVergne, TN USA
13 October 2009
160677LV00003B/228/P